Derrida/Searle

Derrida/Searle

Deconstruction and Ordinary Language

RAOUL MOATI

Translated from the French by
Timothy Attanucci and Maureen Chun

Columbia University Press   New York

Columbia University Press
Publishers Since 1893
New York   Chichester, West Sussex
cup.columbia.edu
Copyright © 2014 Columbia University Press

Library of Congress Cataloging-in-Publication Data
Moati, Raoul.
[Derrida, Searle. English]
Derrida, Searle: deconstruction and ordinary language / Raoul Moati; translated from the French by Timothy Attanucci and Maureen Chun.
   pages cm
Includes bibliographical references and index.
ISBN 978-0-231-16670-6 (cloth: alk. paper) —ISBN 978-0-231-16671-3 (pbk.: alk. paper) —ISBN 978-0-231-53717-9 (e-book)
1. Derrida, Jacques. 2. Searle, John R. 3. Language and languages—Philosophy—20th century. 4. Performative (Philosophy) 5. Speech acts (Linguistics) 6. Ordinary-language philosophy. 7. Deconstruction. 8. Intentionality (Philosophy) I. Title.

B2430.D484M6313   2014
194—dc23

Columbia University Press books are printed on permanent and durable acid-free paper.
This book is printed on paper with recycled content.
Printed in the United States of America
c 10 9 8 7 6 5 4 3 2 1
p 10 9 8 7 6 5 4 3 2 1

Cover design: Noah Arlow

Still confining ourselves for simplicity to *spoken* utterance.
—Austin, *How to Do Things with Words*

Quotations are like robbers by the roadside who make an
armed attack and relieve an idler of his convictions.
—Walter Benjamin, *One-Way Street*

Derrida was bound to be drawn to Austin's discoveries.
—Stanley Cavell, *A Pitch of Philosophy*

Contents

Foreword
Per Formam Doni

Jean-Michel Rabaté

It seems that today, almost ten years after the untimely demise of Jacques Derrida, there are three main ways of approaching his impressive legacy. There is first of all the biographical approach. Since 2010, Benoît Peeters's excellent biography has allowed us to reconsider Derrida's oeuvre in light of his personality. What makes Peeters's biography engaging and refreshing is that we discover a different Derrida, one who appears more driven, tormented, excessive, impassioned than a successful and charismatic world-renowned philosopher. We are surprised to see a neo-Romantic thinker whose vaunting narcissism had to be kept in check and whose power of seduction seemed boundless, yet one with a darker, brooding, melancholy side. He was obsessed by death, his own and that of his loved ones, but stuck until the end to a grueling schedule of international lectures that only an athlete in the physical and intellectual sense could carry through. It was not by chance that Peeters felt the need to publish along with his huge biography a slim volume in which he accounts for the difficulty of such a daunting task.[1] This second book should be made available in English: one should read it side by side with the biography whose author all but disappears and erases his voice to let Derrida speak.

What makes Peeters's biography invaluable is its modesty and the thoroughness of its documentation. Peeters sums up countless letters, manuscripts, and unpublished seminars that one can have access to (which is not always granted) by going to the library of the University of California at Irvine. Thus, for instance, Peeters presents the context of the fifty-two-page letter sent by Derrida to his school friend Pierre Nora, who had published a scathing indictment of the French presence in Algeria. This letter, now added to the republished book by Nora, shows that Derrida sided with Albert Camus and Germaine Tillion, the "liberals" of the time, while remaining uncompromising on issues of ethics and human rights.[2] The debate about the rights of the French colonists to remain in Algeria or even to belong there throws a sharper light on Derrida's otherwise radical politics. This proves that there is a need to know more about Derrida's past "secrets" hidden in his huge archive in which his private life, his theoretical positions, and his ethical and political commitments are intermingled. I would include in this first category the books written by friends and disciples who want to honor his memory, testify to his charisma by making better sense of his ideas. This is the case with books by Nicholas Royle, Peggy Kamuf, Derek Attridge, and Geoffrey Bennington.[3] They attempt to memorialize their mentor and disseminate his teachings while trying not "mourn" him too soon. These four books, written by excellent commentators who have important things to say about aspects of Derrida's theories, hesitate between personal memoirs and textual exegesis. They explain why Derrida is "hard to follow," in all the meanings of the expression.[4] Avoiding the dangers of hagiography, they testify to the pathos of a personal loss while making sense of the French philosopher's lasting legacy.

The second approach is what I would call a systemic interpretation of Derrida's philosophy. It is often provided by authors who were not as close to Derrida as the previous group. They attempt to rethink his concepts and methods from a distance and in their own vocabulary. What they are eager to eschew is the risk of mimetic ventriloquism, a danger faced by all those who grapple with Derrida's idiosyncratic readings of other texts. We see this in Peter Sloterdijk's *Derrida, an Egyptian*,[5] or in Alain Badiou's homage in his *Pocket Pantheon*.[6] Sloterdijk uses thinkers and writers, like Freud, Franz Borkenau, and Niklas Luhmann, to reach a central metaphor in Derrida's oeuvre, which hinges on an inverted Egyptian pyramid. In this way, Derrida becomes, if not immediately a Kafkaian figure, at least a Joseph-like interpreter calling up the hero of a novel by Thomas Mann. Badiou insists on the politics at work in deconstruction, since he chooses to see in Derrida a "man of peace," who destroyed all dichotomies—whether philosophical (like Being and being), racial (like Jew versus Arab), or political (like democracy versus totalitarianism)—in order to reach an instable and fugitive point of undecidability. Key in Derrida's thinking is a productive "indistinction" of distinction, which leads neither to confusion nor to pure difference. Even if there is a huge gap between Badiou's system and Derrida's proliferating texts, they can be joined by a similar concern for the notion of the unde-cidable. A similar but more sustained effort at rethinking the whole system of Derrida's thought has been deployed by Martin Hägglund in his groundbreaking *Radical Atheism*.[7] This book unifies Derrida's project and refutes the idea that Derrida would have moved from a "playful" mode of Nietzschean critique of all foundational concepts to a more "serious," that is, more ethical or even religious, concern with alterity, justice, messianicity, and the dream of a democracy ever "to come." Going back to the earlier insights developed by Derrida when he launched the concept of writing as trace, deferral, and active *différance* in the sense of the creation of a temporal as well as spatial distance, Hägglund posits the logic of "survival" as the keystone of deconstruction. Thus there is only one Derrida, from his first essays to the moving last interview with Jean Birnbaum in 2004,[8] and he is the thinker of a radical finitude, the true heir of Heidegger, and not a Levinassian in disguise.

Finally, a third group of authors discussing Derrida can be called dialogical. They aim at reopening various dialogues between Derrida and other philosophers or writers. The collection edited by John Sal-lis under the title *Deconstruction and Philosophy* provides a good model.[9] Derrida is paired with Hegel, with Heidegger, with Kant, and with Husserl, and contextualized within the discourses of metaphysics and ethics. Derrida appears hence as a "left Heideggerian" (as one would speak of "left Hegelians," including Feuerbach, Stirner, and Marx), that is, as a revolutionary thinker who had the audacity of replacing Heidegger's ontological difference with the "question con-cerning technology." The true audacity consists in using Heidegger's main concepts against themselves. Of course, Derrida had to transform "technology" into "writing," a startling move toward the material, perhaps even toward dialectical materialism, that made a world of difference. If ontological difference can be rewritten as technological difference, writing acquires a new valence, a new violence, and an almost unlimited power in the world of thought and facts. More recently, Leonard Lawlor went to the root of this replacement when he reopened the dossier of Derrida's critique of phenomenology in his superb *Derrida and Husserl*.[10]

It is within this group of dialogical approaches that I see Raoul Moati's elegant book published in 2009 by the Presses Universitaires de France in a series aimed at students, *Derrida/Searle: Déconstruction et langage ordinaire*. Moati is less interested in the genealogy of the confrontation between Derrida and Searle about the true meaning of Austin's theory of the performative—one may note that it is rare to see such polemical ferocity on both sides in a philosophical discussion—than in the general question posed to deconstruction in its dialogue with Anglo-American philosophy of ordinary language. Moati is well equipped for such a task: his interests have roamed freely from Slavoj Žižek to Emmanuel Levinas,[11] and he approaches the discussion opposing Derrida and Searle as dispassionately as possible. He betrays no undue sentimentalism, and he does not bring his personal testimony; in place of a disciple's piety, he displays the candid probity of a true philosophical investigator. This was a prerequisite, since the ground appeared mined due to the fracas, the exchange of insults, and finally an excess of mutual incomprehension. One needs to have sympathy for both camps in order to eschew the effects of transference and countertransference. There is no adulation, adoration, detestation, or denigration of any school here. Moati prefers pointing out Derrida's blind spots and Searle's dead ends to any blind endorsement. Thus Moati insists on Derrida's dependence upon "metaphysical" models that he had been the first to debunk. He sees in Searle a dangerous rejection of the unconscious. This is the condition for an impartial assessment of what we can learn from the debate today.

What is at stake fundamentally is the productivity of the concept of the performative as it was launched by Austin. Moati provides a genealogy of the concept, explaining why its contested legacy was the object of a rivalry, a struggle for appropriation by Derrida and by Searle. Both use the term "intentionality" systematically but with radically different meanings. As Derrida admits in the afterword to *Limited Inc*, he often felt closer to the speech act theory developed by Austin than to the phenomenological tradition he came from: "I sometimes felt, paradoxically, closer to Austin than to a certain Continental tradition from which Searle, on the contrary, has inherited numerous gestures and a logic I try to deconstruct."[12] It was not absurd for Derrida to point to a Husserlian background in Searle, an unthought background of which the American philosopher was blissfully unaware. What Derrida gave us in the end was a more complex and subtle concept of the performative, a concept that could not be limited by reason and social regulation alone, a concept that would not dissolve itself in the aporias of impossible taxonomies, as was the case at the end of Austin's *How to Do Things with Words*. This new dynamism was not lost for innovative thinkers and activists like Judith Butler, who launched her reexamination of sexual difference by using a variation of Derrida's performative. For deconstruction, quite often, the performative tended to relay phenomenology or even rescue it from its endless paradoxes. I have had the opportunity to study the strategic role played by the performative in Derrida's discussion of lies,[13] but this is only one example among many.

Armed with a concept of performativity that will not be "cleaned up" normatively of its constitutive ambiguities and inevitable infelicities, we can learn to think and read better with Derrida. We will read texts more slowly, patiently, posing the foundational questions of framing and context. This will make us move unhesitatingly between genres, at least between the domains of philosophy and literature, both being recharged and re-sourced by a productive dialogue. This will also incite us to take into consideration a longer history of concepts underpinning these debates, debates that will be tackled with more ethical urgency if we do not ignore quasi-immemorial philosophical genealogies. This does not mean that we will have to return endlessly to Plato, whom Derrida called "the master of the perverformative,"[14] but that this long tradition cannot be closed; in fact, it has no closure and should be expanded to engage with other conceptual fields that have been excluded, whether they come from Asia, Africa, or similarly hitherto invisible sources. It is to such a reading program, which consists in bridging the gap between hostile traditions and reawakening the philosophical pulse in all of us, that *Derrida/Searle* invites us. And I, too, invite you, here and now. Is this a performative? When you have finished reading, you will tell me. All I can add is that my invitation is made "per formam doni," that is, in the form of a gift and in the name of friendship, following the legal expression used about the destination of an estate willed by the donor rather than by an operation of the law.

Acknowledgments

I want first to extend my warmest thanks to all those who kindly accompanied, supported, and supervised the development of the present study: Jocelyn Benoist, Marc Crépon, Christiane Chauviré, Ali Benmakhlouf, Sandra Laugier, Charles Ramond, Pierre-François Moreau, Guy-Félix Duportail, Bruno Ambroise, and Pierre-Marie Hasse.

Derrida/Searle

Introduction

The Circumstances of an "Improbable" Debate

At the end of the 1970s, one of the most virulent philosophical disputes known to the contemporary history of ideas erupted between the French philosopher Jacques Derrida, founder of deconstruction, and John R. Searle, American analytic philosopher and theoretician of speech acts.

The confrontation between two major representatives of contemporary philosophy belonging to divergent currents of thought is an event rare enough to arouse attention and awaken curiosity. The unexpected character of such a debate results from the fact that philosophy has rarely, before the twentieth century, appeared as profoundly split into two currents as divergent and irrelevant to each other as continental philosophy and analytic philosophy. Each of these traditions has revealed itself as surprisingly capable of expanding its own space of questions and debates without concern for the problems with which the rival tradition was confronted at the same moment. Given this state of affairs, one can hardly avoid doubts about the actual impact of a philosophical confrontation between two thinkers, each so representative of his own separate philosophical tradition.

At first glance their controversy certainly appears to be a dialogue of the deaf, to the extent that the analytic tools mobilized by the protagonists were rooted in conceptual heritages—phenomenology and psychoanalysis for Derrida, philosophy of logic and the pragmatism of the ordinary for Searle—without any apparent measure of comparison or obvious common points of reference. For this reason, one attempted to explain the difficulty of interpreting the controversy by invoking the nonexistence of theoretical premises common to both thinkers, premises that alone would have assured a dialectical confrontation of the opponents.

Must we therefore resolve to interpret the Derrida/Searle controversy as a symptom of an encounter destined inevitably to failure, incapable of offering the reader anything but the sad spectacle of a violent clash condemned to conceptual sterility? Will we be obliged to categorize this quarrel as one of those curiosities that cause accidental disturbances in the stormy course of the history of ideas before disappearing in the depths of oblivion?

The question of the improbability of such an exchange, of a point of contact between continental and analytic philosophy, is itself one of the central issues raised by the controversy: neither Searle nor Derrida believes that such a debate can "truly take place." This, moreover, is the only point on which the two protagonists of the controversy happen to agree: the insurmountable incompatibility of their respective philosophical approaches. Essentially, everything appears as if the exchange had only taken place to increase the distance between them, "to reiterate the differences" (the title of Searle's reply to Derrida), and thus to reinforce the thesis of a radical absence of any possible consensus.

Indeed, this perspective has predominated in the reception of the debate on both sides of the Atlantic: as an improbable and curious affair, the scale and importance of which deflated like bellows as soon as the initial positions were reestablished. Lacking serenity and calm, the external commentators engaged in the quarrel were desperately lacking in the critical distance required to approach the matter with lucidity and meticulousness.

The present context seems more favorable for this effort; many signs attest to a resurgence of interest in this controversy,[1] allowing us to revisit it today with new interpretative parameters while protecting ourselves from the hasty and impassioned biases that have served too long as a stopgap for an in-depth study of the theoretical issues raised by the controversy itself.

Not wanting to cede too quickly to the temptations of a conciliatory yet hardly rigorous relativism—or to look to this controversy for proof of an insurmountable distance that separates the traditions—I believe that behind the screen of obtuse controversy lies hidden a debate of great conceptual richness. The answers to the questions raised by this debate will no doubt decide the status one should accord to Austin's notion of the "performative."

More than ever before, this debate interrogates the concept of intentionality, the efficacy of its role in accounting for the phenomenon of inscription in the context of enunciation and for the status of the discursive intentions that accompany it. Between the side of phenomenology inherited by deconstruction and the pragmatic side that Searle's speech act theory claims to represent, the debate lays out the richness and diversity of both major traditions of the twentieth century. In order to bring to light the unexpected fecundity of this confrontation of heritages, we must first begin by examining once more the polemic origin of the controversy in which Derrida and Searle were engaged: in "Signature Event Context," Derrida proposes an interpretation of the speech act theory established by the British philosopher John Langshaw Austin at the start of the 1960s in *How to Do Things with Words.*[2] Indeed, Austin's theory of the "performative" constitutes the polemical point of reference around which the entire controversy between Derrida and Searle is constructed.

A little less than ten years after the publication of *HTW* and barely one year after the French translation,[3] Derrida—four years after the publication of the trilogy that inaugurated the adventure of deconstruction[4]—presented a paper (*communication*) to the Congrès International des Sociétés de Philosophie de Langue Française (International Conference of Francophone Philosophical Societies) on the topic of "communication." A revised version of this paper was then published in *Margins of Philosophy* in 1972 under the title "Signature Event Context" (hereafter referred to as "SEC"). This text was translated into English in 1977 by Samuel Weber and Jeffrey Mehlman and published in the journal *Glyph.* In the second issue of 1977, *Glyph* published a reply to Derrida's essay by John Searle—who, it should be remembered, was Austin's student at Oxford and immediately felt it his duty to defend his mentor against Derrida's hack interpretation—

entitled "Reiterating the Differences: A Reply to Derrida."[5] This reply led to a counteroffensive from Derrida in "Limited Inc a b c . . . ," translated by Samuel Weber and published in the same journal, which would become the subject of a book published in the United States and translated two years later in France.[6] Searle refused to give permission for the republication of his essay in this book, and it was not until 1991, with the help of Joëlle Proust, that a translation of Searle's reply was finally available to the French public.[7]

The present study is not concerned with the "second act" of the quarrel, which involved Jonathan Culler's biting essay,[8] Searle's reply to Culler,[9] and finally Derrida's engaged commentary on this confrontation.[10] Derrida found himself once again in the crossfire of Searle's attacks against American deconstruction—of which Culler is one representative—which his work and teachings had inspired across the Atlantic.

Given the relative neglect of this debate in current philosophical discussions, it seems more opportune to explain as thoroughly as possible the divergent conceptual logic employed by Derrida and Searle in the seminal essays of their controversy.

A HERITAGE DISPUTE: INTRODUCTION TO A VIOLENT EXCHANGE

The Derrida/Searle encounter should be situated in its own particular context: a violent polemic over Austin.

In light of what Searle interprets as an inadmissible appropriation of his mentor's theory, one can understand the extreme brutality of his reply to Derrida's "SEC." Searle in no way aims to open a dialogue with an adversary, but tends instead to ridicule him by out-lining, with a serrated argumentative knife, the ineptitude and inco-herence of his interpretation of Austin. Claiming an unassailable affiliation with Austin, Searle wants to defend the Oxford theoreti-cian and protect his theory from the hack version given by Derrida's deconstructive analysis.

According to Searle, it is necessary to disabuse oneself of the illu-sion that the Derridean reading of Austin may lead to an encoun-ter between continental and analytic philosophical traditions. The Derridean departitioning remains superficial. The hermetic purity and unique complexity of analytic philosophy should not be altered by the whims of the nonbeliever: "It would be a mistake, I think, to regard Derrida's discussion of Austin as a confrontation between two prominent philosophical traditions."[11] Searle adopts the tone of mockery and not of a rational polemic; he demonstrates his will to expose Derrida's analysis of Austin as a sequence of mis-interpretations to an Anglo-Saxon world that finds itself more and more seduced by deconstruction. The concern here is to dis-close the far-fetched rambles of this new avatar of obscurantism called deconstruction, which may sparkle all it wants as long as it stops laying claim to a field of research whose scope easily exceeds its competence.

According to this view, Derrida has thus not understood Austin at all, and his misreading must be explained by the fundamental obscurity that envelops his arguments: "I should say at the outset that I did not find his arguments very clear and it is possible that I may have misinterpreted him as profoundly as I believe he has misinterpreted Austin."[12] On the Derridean side, the reply to Searle's reply is no less marked by irony and mockery. The questions raised by deconstruction are mobilized at first to ridicule the adversary. This practice, Derrida claims, falls in line with the very spirit of the deconstructive approach. At the same time, the mocking tone, which can surprise the unsuspecting reader, upsets the proper atmosphere of academic discourse.

The question of the status of Searle's reply is at issue, and through it the identity of its author: "And I shall place in the margin (I ask the publishers to follow this recommendation) the following question. I address it to Searle. But where is he? Do I know him?"[13] This question becomes all the more pressing, considering that Searle added a copyright to his reply, that is, a legal seal related to a signature, revealing a desire for exclusive possession of his written works. Polemicizing with brio, though, Derrida plays with the reply and its author: for him, this game has the value of deconstructive argumentation. Indeed, Derrida does not understand why Searle, who accuses him of saying things about Austin that are "obviously false" (it being implicitly understood that he alone, John R. Searle, possesses the truth about Austin), needs to stick a copyright on his text. If Searle is fundamentally right, if he represents what is "obviously true," his reply is no longer his own. But, inversely, if Searle feels that his reply does not tell the "obvious truth," it becomes all the more necessary to sign it, knowing all the while that this signature exposes his own doubt about his capacity to say what is "obviously true."

The presence of the copyright reveals the inherent ambiguity of all signatures: signing serves to mark presence, but this mark is only necessary to the extent that it is based on the precariousness of all presence, the ineluctable threat of its own dissipation; the mark thus bears witness to the bankruptcy of all presence and, by the same stroke, silences all opposing arguments.[14]

Moreover, Derrida devotes his attention to the acknowledgments contained in Searle's reply, where he thanks Hubert Dreyfus and David Searle ("This is the first note of the Reply"). This exposes a second contradiction in the use of the copyright, that of the improbability of the exclusive paternity of Searle's reply. The copyright is here revelatory of a fractured signature, of an argument that escapes even Searle. The copyright bears witness to a misappropriation that renders the intended integrity of the author of this reply more than improbable.

Derrida also reacts to Searle's words concerning his commentary of Austin: "The confrontation never quite takes place." Derrida is astonished by the virulence of the reaction from Searle and his allies, covered under the same copyright: Why rise to reestablish the good Austinian word if the confrontation never took place? Why propose a confrontation over a confrontation that never took place?[15]

Unable to identify his opponent since it remains unclear how many people are behind Searle's reply, Derrida decides to resort to a legal vocabulary that he diverts from usual usage in order to give the author of the reply the title of "More or Less Limited Liability Company" [*société plus ou moins anonyme*].[16] Searle thus becomes "Sarl" in the reply to the reply, which, in the spirit of deconstructive argumentation, increases the irony of the text.[17]

Derrida admits that there is a sentence in Searle's reply that he is ready to agree with: "It would be a mistake, I think, to regard Derrida's discussion of Austin as a confrontation between two prominent philosophical traditions." Derrida indeed denies wanting to represent any philosophical tradition here at all. On the contrary, he claims to be part of a philosophical connivance with Austin and asserts that it is his right to reclaim the heritage of the Oxford philosopher. If there is a heritage, it certainly does not derive for Derrida from a sectarian alliance that valorizes one tradition over another, but from a destabilization of borders between traditions that a new reading of Austin's philosophy would make possible: "Among the many reasons that make me unqualified to represent a 'prominent philosophical tradition,' there is this one: I consider myself to be in many respects quite close to Austin, both interested in and indebted to his problematic."[18] This testimony to his proximity to Austin is equivalent to defending a deconstructive interpretation of the British philosopher's theory as fully legitimate. This interpretation would result in blurring the supposedly strict partitioning that the respective holders of each tradition present as insurmountable.

Revisited by deconstruction, Austin appears to belong to the history of Western philosophy in its unconscious adherence to the metaphysical presuppositions that have driven it since Plato.[19] Drawing upon all the consequence of such a paradox, Derrida is led to wonder: "isn't Sarl ultimately more continental and Parisian than I am? I shall try to show why. Sarl's premises and method are derived from continental philosophy, and in one form or another they are very present in France. If I may cite myself, for the last time referring to a text other than *Sec* (hereafter I will restrict myself to the latter essay), this is what I wrote in 'Avoir l'oreille de la philosophie' [To Have the Ear of Philosophy] . . . : '*Signature Event Context* analyzes the metaphysical premises of the Anglo-Saxon—and fundamentally moralistic—theory of the performative, of speech acts or discursive events. In France, it seems to me that these premises underlie the hermeneutics of Ricoeur and the archaeology of Foucault.'"[20] In the preamble to his reply, Derrida seeks to understand with what authority Searle is in a position to decide what, in "SEC," is understood or misunderstood about Austin, and what is to be accepted or rejected.

What right does Searle have, after the series of profound distortions to which he submitted Austin's speech act theory, to proclaim himself the Oxford philosopher's exclusive heir, the only one to hold the right to commentary and the rehabilitation of the word of his mentor? And, more shocking still, the only one to grant himself the right to critique and improve the theory.

According to Derrida, "Sarl would like to be Austin's sole legitimate heir *and* his sole critic."[21] Yet Derrida accepts that it is not his prerogative to say what is true about Austin: a theoretician attentive to *speech acts* should have, out of fidelity to the Austinian dismantling of the truth/falsehood fetish, asked himself whether the real aim of a text like "SEC" was the *truth* about Austin.

The performative dimension is, on the contrary, completely accepted by Derrida, such that "SEC" as a speech act could have said "something apparently 'false'" or doubtful while still presenting it in such a way, with such a form or turn of phrase (trapped or parasitic), that the debate has a greater chance of getting started and the self-authorized descendants of this *prominent* philosophical tradition cannot help but answer back. This could also be a deconstructive performance: proposing a text that, by its very indeterminate existence, "defines at every moment the oppositions of concepts or of values, the rigor of those oppositional limits that speech act theory endorses by virtue of its very axiomatics."[22]

However, this parasitic method of approaching "SEC" and Searle's reply—through the ironic and indirect treatment of the latter—is disabled as soon as the exultant preamble is over. Not that Derrida has renounced the deconstruction of the border between serious and nonserious utterances, but the reply henceforth demands that he respond in turn point by point to the substance of the theoretical issues.[23]

Before going into the details of Searle's replies to Derrida and vice versa, let us return to the text that provoked a response from Searle and constitutes the center of the dispute, "SEC," and to the renewed approach to Austin it has initiated.

I

The Iterative as the Reverse Side of the Performative

"SEC" opens with an epigraph from Austin's *How to Do Things with Words*: "Still confining ourselves for simplicity to *spoken* utterance."

This reference/reverence to the Austinian text is surprising, considering the first lines of Derrida's text: we observe that the topic broached by Derrida, if it approaches the problem of enunciation [*énonciation*],[1] is not entirely equivalent to it since Derrida proposes to take *communication* as his object of analysis.

We thus notice a slippage from the notion of *enunciation* to the notion of *communication*, which presents no small number of difficulties. The strangest point here is that such slippage finds its counterpart in analytic philosophy, and more particularly in Searle, who, we will see, *also* rereads Austin's theory starting from the framework of communication, which he takes from Paul Grice.[2] We thus witness how the protagonists, Searle as much as Derrida, take the linguistics of enunciation defended by Austin toward a theory of *communication* that the Oxford philosopher never maintained—and this without their noticing at any point in the dispute that they are submitting Austin's thought to the same distortion. (This is also the case for the commentators of the quarrel in both the United States and France.)

It is surprising to observe that Derrida, who had no familiarity with Grice, was himself also led to fit Austin's theory into the mold of communication. For this reason, to which we will return, convergences arise in the background between Searle and Derrida, unbeknown to them. Indeed, we will see how the Searlean critique of Grice is applied to the Derridean framework without the constant of communication being questioned for a single moment during the entire duration of the controversy.

This constant is the common measure implicit in their confrontation. There is therefore, and we will return to this again, *a common denominator* to their antagonism: following Austin, Derrida and Searle propose two divergent conceptions *of the same phenomenon*: communication. It is thus not at all certain that our two authors are blowing hot air in a pointless polemic filled with insults without philosophical basis. Quite the contrary, there are in fact two conceptions of the intentionality of communication at stake: on the one hand, for Derrida, an intentionality of communication inspired by phenomenological intentionality, and on the other, for Searle, an intentionality of communication taken from Grice's pragmatism. Between continental philosophy and analytic philosophy, a bridge emerges, attesting to a whole swath of questions common to both traditions at the same moment of their development, but dealt with using apparently incommensurable conceptual tools. Let us recall that, according to Derrida's own account, "SEC" was "a communication to the Congrès international des Sociétés de philosophie de langue française, Montreal, August 1971. The theme of the colloquium was 'Communication.'"[3] Employing the *mise en abîme* effects particular to the deconstructive approach, Derrida plays with the different meanings of the word "communication" that his text solicits. "Communication" represents at once the theme of the colloquium at which Derrida was participating as well as the genre of his remarks: it is a communication (oral remarks, a conference talk) on communication (the theme of the colloquium). Despite having the allure of cute rhetoric, such circularity is the spring that drives Derridean argumentation: indeed, it is not certain that the concept of communication can emerge unscathed. The *mise en abîme* allows Derrida to put the word "communication" to the test of its proper definition: Derrida asks if the *word* "communication" proves capable of corresponding fully to its proper concept—put differently, if it *communicates a determined meaning*. The concept of communication does describe a movement of meaning, that of the transmission of a content from a speaker to an interlocutor through the intermediary of language. Yet the transmission of a meaning is itself only possible if each word is attached to a univocal signified, in other words, only on the condition that the stability of semantics is acknowledged: "Is it certain that there corresponds to the word *communication* a unique, univocal concept, a concept that can be rigorously grasped and transmitted: a communicable concept?"[4] It is this very presumption of stability that deconstruction seeks to undermine: since the definition of communication can be maintained only if each word has a univocal signification, to prove that the word "communication" is intrinsically ambiguous is to demonstrate that it cannot maintain its own definition—the transmission of meaning from a sender to a receiver—without contradicting itself.

"SEC" thus begins by interrogating not the notion of communication, but the a priori possibility of a stable attachment of the signifier to the signified. If this is undone by the ambiguity of the word "communication," the entire system of communication defined by the linguistic sciences will then break down.

OVERCOMING SEMANTICS THROUGH FORCE:
PROLEGOMENA TO THE APORETIC DIMENSION
OF THE DERRIDA/AUSTIN CONNECTION

The semantic sense of communication thus appears restrictive, since it considers the univocality of meaning as the condition of communication even though the very signifier *communication* causes such univocality to vacillate by opening onto nonsemantic meanings of communication. In disclosing the force of repression in the work's semantic theories of language, Derrida proposes to liberate the polysemy suppressed in the word "communication":

> To the semantic field of the word *communication* belongs the fact that it also designates nonsemantic movements. Here at least provisional recourse to ordinary language and to the equivocalities of natural language teaches us that one may, for example, *communicate a movement*, or that a tremor, a shock, a displacement of *force* can be communicated—that is, propagated, transmitted. It is also

said that different or distant places can communicate between each other by means of a given passageway or opening. What happens in this case, what is transmitted or communicated, *are not phenomena of meaning or signification.*[5]

Derrida's demonstration already points implicitly in the direction of Austin's theory; Derrida makes mention of a "provisional recourse to ordinary language and to the equivocalities of natural language" in order to reject the relevance of a purely semantic approach to communication. Austin's philosophy sets out to establish a theory that would no longer interrogate meaning *for itself* as a detached *(thing) in itself,* but would describe its dependence on our uses of language in circumstances determined by our ordinary recourse to them. According to Austin, because these uses are maintained by conventions, they guarantee our rational employment of language.

The philosophy of ordinary language would thus offer an alternative path to the semanticism of the linguistic sciences, since it is quite true that Austin sought a description of the phenomenon of enunciation based on the fact that it is not reducible to the transmission of a meaning detached from the ordinary circumstances of its production. In *How to Do Things with Words*, Austin begins with a critique of the "truth/falsehood fetish" and opens his analysis with a description of one category of acts systematically neglected by philosophical and traditional linguistic theories that are nonetheless omnipresent in our ordinary practices of language: performative acts.

The typological description of performative acts allows him to relativize the semantic approach to language, to the advantage of an analytic of *force* constitutive of the *pragmatic value* of enunciations. The meaning of words for Austin does not exist as a *stable content* of the sign independent of its use. From the perspective of ordinary language, the univocality of utterances or their terms is thus not a given: to understand their signification, it is necessary to relate them to their use in established circumstances. In other words, the question of meaning *posed for itself* proves nothing if it remains centered on the signification of words detached from the actual circumstances of the *production* of the enunciation. This opens the analysis to the terrain of the *performative force* that presides over the realization of the meaning of linguistic acts. Performative acts are characterized by the fact that their function is not to describe a state of the world, but to allow *action in the world* through the intermediary of words: promising, asking, warning, and informing are performative acts that accomplish actions through the relevant use of language. For this reason, they draw upon a linguistic value irreducible to semantic criteria of truth. Their value is *pragmatic*, and they have their own grammar that belongs to what Austin calls the "illocutionary" as well as specific conditions of success that Austin names "felicity." The illocutionary value permits the identification of the *force* that presides over the realization of a performative linguistic act. The specificity of speech acts, insofar as they belong to a general field of action and use *force*, is the production of certain *effects* in the world and on other persons to whom we are speaking. The world described by Austin is thus not only the natural world composed of brute facts, but also a world full of conventions that validate the realization of acts of normative import (such as speech acts). For this reason, Austin distinguishes within the performative two types of inassimilable acts, each accomplished by the deployment of a *distinct* force that it sets in motion: on the one hand, the illocutionary act that has a properly *conventional* efficiency; and on the other, the perlocutionary act that has a simply *natural* efficiency. It is precisely this duality that immediately escapes the Derridean description of nonsemantic communication (the transmission of a "force" rather than a "meaning"). Indeed, Derrida assimilates these two types of activity to a single *natural force.* The problematic of force mobilized by Austin, on the contrary, is broken down into two types of efficiency, each irreducible to the other.

When a promise is made, the illocutionary act has the *effect* of committing the speaker to the interlocutor to whom the promise was made. This effect is the result of a force, but this force *is intrinsic* to the *conventional* value of the act; there could be no promise if this value did not commit one person to another. On the other hand, the per-locutionary act accomplished *at the same time* as the illocutionary act but on a distinct ontological plane—that of natural effectiveness—introduces a force that has nothing conventional about it, and is more a matter of the *extrinsic* result of the act, produced as the *natural effect* on the interlocutor at the receiving end. If one can anticipate the effects of the illocutionary force, which is analytically deducible from the essence of the act, one cannot predict the perlocutionary force to the extent that its terrain of fulfillment is underneath the act, on the side of the feelings engendered in the interlocutor. Therefore, fears, emotions, and excitations are so many perlocutionary phenomena *inassimilable* to the conventional commitment implicated by the act itself. Whether or not the way in which an individual makes a prom-ise inspires respect and confidence, the promise does not commit the speaker any less to the person to whom the promised is made: the perlocutionary efficiency remains contingent on the conventional scenario of the act, which, for its part, implies commitment *systematically*. It is also clear, for example, that in order to insult someone it would be necessary, beyond the conventional use of certain words to accomplish such an act, that the person feel insulted, but this feeling is not deducible analytically from the act and is never implicated systematically by it.

Austin's order of pragmatic forces remains the component that escapes the intelligence of "SEC," and it is on this point that Searle criticizes Derrida's essay with excessive vigor. From the first page of "SEC," it becomes apparent that Derrida has created confusion between two levels of force that Austin considers categorically dissimilar. This crucial distinction in the Austinian system is voided by the dualism Derrida introduces between meaning and natural force, and this *to the detriment* of the force of convention. Indeed, when Derrida evokes the "nonsemantic movements" produced by language, he affirms that "*a movement*, or . . . a tremor, a shock, a displacement of *force* can be communicated—that is, propagated, transmitted."[6]

The misunderstanding between the philosophy of ordinary language and deconstruction finds here its matrix of intelligibility: Derrida praises Austin further for managing to emancipate his approach to language from the truth/falsehood fetish by substituting it with the sole reality of "force." Derrida adheres, however, to an *exclusively naturalist and voluntarist conception of force* and abandons entirely the conventional aspect of illocutionary force, on which Austin's analysis rests.

On the other hand, it is important to note here that for Grice the pragmatic (illocutionary) value of utterance depends on the *communication of an intention in the perlocutionary act.* In other words, for Grice as well as for Derrida's truncated understanding of Austin, we find the imbrication of the illocutionary and perlocutionary registers of utterance. Starting with the critique of the confusion of these registers—which he first notices in Grice—Searle forges his own theory of speech acts faithful to the Austinian divide between the illocutionary and the perlocutionary. It is thus entirely logical that he is driven to challenge Derrida and to revive the attacks initially formulated in opposition to Grice.

FROM COMMUNICATION TO "DISSEMINATION"

Derrida's argument tends to show the existence of a meaning of the word "communication" that reveals a wholly *natural* dimension of communication, independent of communication's semantic functioning. Indeed, Derrida pursues his analysis thus: "What happens in this case, what is transmitted or communicated, *are not phenomena of meaning or signification.* In these cases we are dealing neither with a semantic or conceptual content, nor with a semiotic operation, and even less with a linguistic exchange."[7]

The goal of the argumentation here is to show the difficulty of deciding between two senses of the term. For one could legitimately ask what privilege of semantics would allow one meaning of "communication" to take precedence over the other. It is precisely here that the entire difficulty arises: by privileging an exclusively semantic meaning of "communication," the structural theories transgress the equivocation of the word "communication" in order to reattach it to a privileged univocal context from which all the others derive secondarily. The reduction of semantic plurality proceeds with sudden force that aims to contain the indefinite process of meaning as an escape by means of an *arbitrary* decision to stabilize the value of signs. Inversely, the semantic equivocality of the word "communication" (and the general regime of signs) compromises every project to stabilize meaning: "the value of literal, *proper meaning* appears more problematical than ever," affirms Derrida.[8] From the point of view of deconstruction, it is a metaphysical illusion to claim that one may surmount the semantic erring of the signs of language (even once they are contextualized, as is the case here for the word "communication"). The ambiguity is in fact revelatory of the *undecidable* character of the meaning of words, to the extent that such ambiguity comes from the more profound process of *dissemination* that deconstruction intends to exhume from metaphysical repression.

The problematic of "SEC" is inscribed in the wheels of this dialectic opposing dissemination to the presumed stability of meaning determined by the context of the enunciation. The reference to context is also a result of the pretension to contain the disseminating hemorrhage of meaning through the attribution of a value to the enunciation produced in certain circumstances. This claim is deconstructed by Derrida in the name of a dissemination capable of exploding the contextual framework in which, for lack of a stable content, the utterance would discover a meaning that could be attributed to it *hic et nunc*. From the point of view of deconstruction, the context also reveals itself to be traversed by instability. The indeterminacy striking the regime of signifiers applies equally to contextualization and comes to contaminate it from within, to the point of destroying its claims to fix a pragmatic value (illocutionary or perlocutionary) to the performative. For Derrida, a link exists between semantic unde-cidability and contextual indeterminacy, two problems that would have *writing* as a common symptom.

WRITING: THE FRAGMENTATION OF COMMUNICATION

The issue of the section that follows, entitled "Writing and Telecom-munication," asks if writing is or is not a means of communication. Does writing ensure the transmission of the content of meaning undamaged? To all appearances, this is the case, as Derrida writes: "If one takes the notion of writing in its usually accepted sense—which above all does not mean an innocent, primitive, or natural sense—one indeed must see it as a *means of communication.*"[9]

According to this conception, writing ensures, in the same capac-ity as speech, *the transmission of the content of meaning* from a sender to a receiver, and this without the message having been affected by the written sign authorized at its transmission. The difficulty mani-fested by this conception resides in the presupposed lack of distinc-tion between the regimes of speech and writing; both seem capable of fulfilling the task of transmitting meaning in the same way and with-out there being any need to question the difference between the two modalities. The transition from oral communication to written com-munication—which implies the *material inscription* of the message and its maintenance beyond the moment of its production—does not affect in any way the mechanism of the communicative transmission. On the contrary, affirms Derrida, "One must even acknowledge [writing] as a powerful means of communication which *extends* very far, if not infi-nitely, the field of oral or gestural communication."[10] For the partisans of communicative writing, writing ensures the extension in time and space of "oral or gestural communication." In other words, writing amounts to the undamaged relay of face-to-face communication.

Such a system is thus necessarily built on a *continualist and isomorphic* conception of writing. For this, writing employs a power of communication *identical to that* of concrete speech and gesture. To write, moreover, is thus to communicate without the concrete presence of a speaker but without this presence having disappeared in the *transition* from orality or gesture to writing, because writing represents its spatial and temporal extension, its expanded continuation. Writing in this scenario becomes the paradoxical expression of orality or gesture, that is to say, of a source of emission continually present and, at the same time, *indifferent* to the effective existence of its author. It represents, in other words, *the paradoxical extension of the presence of the speaker despite his absence or his disappearance*. The aporia of the communicative conception of writing resides in this paradox. For, as Derrida explains, the rupture in the transition from orality to writing must itself have been deactivated in order to ensure for writing a communicative capacity *identical to that of speech*.[11] Writing sees itself reduced to the role of an offshoot of oral communication, and occupies the function of representative by extension. In order to be considered a means of communication, writing must be inscribed in the direct continuation of voice or gesture while employing the same powers of transmission that permit it to overcome the deficiency caused by the absence of sender in written communication.

In writing, an inevitable scission is created between the moment of the emission of a message and its transmission, which are contemporaneous in oral or gestural communication but are absolutely no longer so in the case of a text that could have been written several centuries ago, and of which there remains only writing, *detached* from the presence of its producer. This *noncontemporaneousness* of intention with respect to signs formerly mobilized within presence represents the *specificity* of writing. This specificity remains *unthought* by the communicational theory of writing, which illusorily conceives of written communication as the *continuation of oral communication*.[12] The limited range of oral or gestural communication is expanded and thereby benefits from an unlimited communicational efficiency capable of transcending the borders circumscribed by the actual presence of the speaker in speech or in gesture without, however, compromising the realization of the process of communication. In the case of written communication, the absence of the speaker/sender no longer represents a procedural defect that harms communication. On the contrary, "meaning, the content of the semantic message, is thus transmitted, *communicated*, by different *means*, by technically more powerful mediations, over a much greater distance," and this takes place, Derrida specifies, "within a homogenous element across which the unity and integrity of meaning is not affected in an essential way. Here, all affection is accidental."[13] Indeed, even when the very elementary conditions of communication—principally the actual presence of the speaker—are no longer fulfilled, this does not affect in any way the transmissibility of a message once the dramatic increase in communicational efficiency that comes with writing is accorded to speech as well. In this way communication belongs to the "homogeneous element" of continuous presence, and ensures the ideal extension of voice and of gesture in writing. Communication is reattached to the element of ideal uninterrupted presence, independent of the actual presence of the speaker/sender. This presence is no longer required for the realization of communication henceforth maintained by the continuous present of the ideal presence liberated from the "grammar" of the empirical present and from its inherent ontological fragility (nonpermanence, spatiotemporal localization, *hic et nunc* determination and disappearance).

We can observe here the tension between two modalities of the present, which had already served as the primary subject of Derrida's first works on Husserl, identified in his introduction to *The Origin of Geometry*. In this text, Husserl made the objectivity of original acts dependent on the constitution of geometric idealities, on the possibility of their transmission in time through the mediation of writing. Husserl considers the phenomenological "reactivation" as the cognitive means of allowing transcendental consciousness to access original acts of constitution maintained in the present by their scriptural transmission.[14] In the Derridean text that concerns us here, we find the same mistrust with respect to the supposed ideal integrity of the present of presence in writing. This configuration is unacceptable to the extent that it supposes that writing permits the spatial and historical preservation of the intentional permanence of the distant speaker/sender in space or in time, if formerly living. Written communication has the virtue of *abolishing* all distance, spatial as well as temporal, between the sender and the receiver. It realizes the feat of guaranteeing the continuity of presence despite all obstacles, of sustaining in the *present* the speaker's message without his disappearance affecting the full integrity of his act of communicating something, which remains universally present, at anyone's disposal at any place or any time. According to this conception, moreover, writing succeeds in abstracting presence from its initial empiricism in order to preserve its timeless and eternal form, the ideal kernel transmissible as an *intended meaning* [*vouloir-dire*],[15] as the ideal presence of an act of thinking sustained and archived beyond its actual carrier. Oral communication thus no longer knows any limit, it overcomes in the oneness of sustained presence the disturbances of empirical separation, it succeeds in establishing its universal hold on writing by undoing the inherent finitude of all concrete speech. The maintained presence of the present act of meaning to say something presupposes that the "present" is put in a privileged temporal position: the present is no longer a temporal mode distinct from the past and from the future, and becomes the transcendental mode that allows the *temporalization* of the past and the future. At the level of written communication, the past of the sign, previously mobilized by a speaker now gone, could not be understood unless as a form of the "present past" for the receiving consciousness that grasps it by opening up to the original intended meaning of its sender. This violence inflicted on the finitude of presence, transformed into a continuous and eternal present of the sending presence, derives from the metaphysical restriction of writing that Derrida names "logocentrism." This logocentrism amounts to the reduction of temporality to the dimension in which, benefiting from the eternal present of the spirit's timeless provisions, a receiving consciousness is given access to the living and present consciousness of the sender, with the effect that all origins of meaning that cannot be systematically recuperated at a later time are denied and negated. The present of consciousness thus becomes the "homogenous element" of phonetic communication, the operator of the generalized communicability of meaning from one age to another, all ages being holders of a Humanity conscious of its ideally self-continuous presence in the transhistorical hypostasis of speech. The actual diversity finds its point of unification in the ideally uniform presence of the present of speech, capable of overcoming the obstacles to the establishment of universal communication, at the price of the exclusion of all forms of temporal alterity—of nonpresence—from the field of philosophical investigation.

According to this conception, lacking the actual presence of a speaker, writing continues to express *his intentional presence*. Freed from its spatiotemporal limitations, phonetic expression deposited in writing allows the sender to be *always there* despite his absence, in effect, his death. This sender continues to *mean* something and arrive at his intentions; his voice continues to resonate and make itself heard across the written remnant of its presence that is nonetheless dissipated. The preservation of this intentional presence of the sender—the supposed atemporality of his *intended meaning*—detached from his actual presence is not at all evident for Derrida: this preservation is revelatory of a metaphysics ruled by the paradigm of speech to the detriment of writing. The hypostasis of writing, by which this metaphysics is ruled as the metaphysics of presence, remains for Derrida a reassuring myth destined to conjure *the test of death*, which, unbeknown to itself, always plagues all speech despite its exaggerated claim to maintain itself in a stable self-transparence. Deconstruction takes as its objective the reintroduction of the suppressed element of writing, compared in many of Derrida's texts to the Freudian death drive. By recognizing a mortifying textuality in the upper reaches of speech, one may *deconstruct* the phonological centrality of metaphysics and suppress the theme of writing as the *absence* and *irreversible loss* of the continuous presence of *intended meaning*. The deconstructive approach thus proposes to destabilize, from within, the "logocentric" system inherent in metaphysics as a metaphysics of presence and the resulting sterile conception of writing.

To present and reverse this thesis, Derrida relies here on the paradigmatic example of Condillac's theory in *Essay on the Origin of Human Knowledge*. In the *Essay*, Derrida tells us, "the origin and function of writing is placed, in a kind of noncritical way, *under the authority of the category of communication*."[16] In this text, Condillac retraces the genesis of writing as a supplementary stage in the elaboration and perfection of communication. To communicate, for Condillac, means to transmit a mental content or idea. Writing does not represent a rupture in the line of communication—the passage from the presence of the speaker to his absence—but on the contrary its full realization, a supplementary degree of achievement in its historical process of perfection. Writing, in the Condillacian sense, "will never have the least effect on the structure and content of the meaning (of ideas) that it will have to vehiculate. The same content, previously communicated by gestures and sounds, henceforth will be transmitted by writing."[17] In addition, despite the increasing complexity of the system of written signs, from pictographic writing to hieroglyphic and ideographic and finally alphabetic writing, the same constant structures the evolution/increasing complexity of writing, namely, its *representational value*. Writing, whatever form it takes, has as its structuring characteristic the representation of a mental content or idea, in the same way as gestures or words uttered in speech. For Condillac, the representation of content constitutes a property of linguistic communication that finds in writing a supplementary resource and continuation of oral or gestural expression.[18] What is remarkable in the Condillacian approach, which according to Derrida is representative of the philosophical approach to writing in general, is the preservation of the integrity of communicational efficiency from orality to writing, despite the passage from locutionary presence to its absence. The absence of the sender in writing does not affect the communicational system described by Condillac. According to Derrida, however, this absence must logically introduce a discontinuity in the transmission of contents. The Condillacian conception of writing reveals its inability to conceive absence in its own radical terms, as something other than a derivative avatar of presence. The absence of a speaker in written words remains the great forgotten element in the history of metaphysics, which conceives absence only in the form of a "modification of presence." Yet, contrary to speech uttered in the present, in the presence of the sender and the receiver, the moment of writing is that of an ineluctable split for the author to the extent that the signs that he constructs are bound to survive him *beyond his living intention* to signify something with them. Inversely, for Condillac, the trace continues to be considered the offshoot of oral expression. In our experience of speech, signifiers appear so unified with expression that they end up giving the impression of adding nothing to it, maintaining the speaker in a continuous self-presence that continues the intimate relation to the self characterizing the inner life of the soul, subtracted from the world and from all forms of alterity. Words begin to signify to the extent that they appear transfigured into contents of meaning by the present thought that summons them. This summons engenders the metaphysical illusion of the complete adherence of words to the thought that invests them with a continuation of itself, extended through them, but in spite of them and their possible scriptural rupture with the economy of presence.

The application of the model of speech to written communication allows the resolution of the aporia by universalizing the homogenous regime of present speech, where speech believes it has nothing to do with anything but itself. It makes one forget its capacity to cause fractures, to defer words, as well as their continuing aptitude to be remobilized in writing in a process detached from the mental life of their author. The experience of speech generalized and applied to writing thus allows us to set aside, as a plausible hypothesis, the sign's capacity for detachment in relation to the present moment in which we mobilize it in thought, and in which its survival beyond presence appears to dissipate and the possibility of writing as absence fades. In speech, thought thus presents itself as the reassuring face of unfailing unity, preserved from all distance from itself, from all difference between its substance and the signs that it animates.

Voice purifies signifiers of any vague desire to dissent from presence; it undoes, once it is philosophically hypostasized, all possibility of dissidence in relation to the unfailing continuation of the unified and unifying present of thought present to itself. This is what Derrida describes in *Positions*: the voice as the experience of the dissolution of the signifying regime into the self-presence of conscious utterance. Since the signifier is not exclusively the instrument of speech, *since it can always become writing*, only the impression of its erasure allows us to imagine it unfailingly unified with the self-presence of thought:

When I speak, not only am I conscious also of keeping as close as possible to my thought, or to the "concept," a signifier that I hear as soon as I emit it, that seems to depend upon my pure and free spontaneity, requiring the use of no instrument, no accessory, no force taken from the world. Not only do the signifier and the signified seem to unite, but also, in this confusion, the signifier seems to erase itself or to become transparent, in order to allow the concept to present itself as what it is, referring to nothing other than its presence. The exteriority of the signifier seems reduced.[19]

Voice thus gives the reassuring impression of dissolving the duality of presence and signifiers. Yet this totalizing resolution presupposes the repression of the possibility of writing as the survival of signifiers beyond the living presence of the speaker who employs them.

For Derrida, however, to conceptualize or "think" writing [*penser l'écriture*] is to come to terms with the split of sign and presence, to accept the dissemination of the sign as it extends beyond the present state of control. The realization of the split inherent to writing attracts no theoretical attention from Condillac: indeed, "according to him, to trace means 'to express,' 'to represent,' 'to recall,' 'to make present.'"[20] For Condillac, writing is defined as a communicational medium of the same order as speech: "writing is a species of this general communication."[21] In Condillacian metaphysics, writing does not have an epistemological status distinct from that of speech; it is simply a mode derived from speech in the homogenous element of communication, and thus remains *phonetic* writing.

Derrida is concerned with the deconstruction of this accepted sense in order to rethink at fresh expense—something that is new to philosophy—writing in its properly paradoxical phenomenality. This redefinition necessarily implies a loosening of ties between writing and communication. Indeed, Derrida tells us, what characterizes the written sign in the first place is that it "is proffered in the absence of the addressee."[22] The absence that must be thought proves irreducible to a modified form of presence. Thus the deflation of presence introduced by writing must be conceived as something other than the restrictive form of a loss that may be compensated (where the original thought could be, thanks to the graphic preservation of the sign, eternally grasped in its purity of origin without damage).

On the contrary, a true phenomenology of writing must be able to grasp its object from the *absolute dimension of absence*. It is precisely in this dimension that its *condition of legibility* resides. Indeed, the text remains legible despite and beyond the disappearance of its author or receiver. Put differently, the legibility of the text *functions independently of the presence of its author or its receiver*. A text written by an author henceforth dead *remains legible* even if it is no longer read by anyone. In addition, the text is *detachable* from the context of communication to which it was first ascribed, that is to say that it can always be *repeated* in circumstances that are no longer the initial circumstances of the communication. The legibility of the text reveals itself indifferent to the communicational parameters (context, speaker, receiver, message) to which it had been ascribed *at first*. The intention to communicate something in writing fades into its legibility, *which persists once communication is complete*, once the initial conditions of the semantic transmission disappear. This is why "it must be repeatable—iterable—in the absolute absence of the addressee or of the empirically determinable set of addressees."[23] Indeed, the text is not legible only once; it remains so indefinitely, including in circumstances that are no longer at all those of its initial production, that do not maintain any relation with the circumstances of its original communicational aim: "A writing that was not structurally legible—iterable—beyond the death of the addressee would not be writing."[24] The legibility of the text is not dependent on its communicational function since the text remains legible, including for those to whom it was not originally addressed.

The legibility of the text is defined less by the message it was to transmit initially, and thus by the intention that drives it, than by a *constitutive iterability*. The difference between speech and text resides in the ever-possible liberation of the text from the horizon of communication and its intentions. The legibility of the text overflows and liberates itself from its original intended meaning. In other words, the text continues to be readable independently of the localized meaning that it assumes in a determined context of communication. For this reason, semantic transmission represents only a *precarious and limited moment of legibility*, no longer its privileged mode of operation. Writing does not serve as the *medium* of the transmission of meaning, but exhibits well before then, for those who understand its specific movement, the intimate test of death that traverses every linguistic performance in the form of an inevitable loss of self-proximity, without the hope of compensation.

THE PROBLEM OF INTENTIONAL PRESENCE

We understand now the importance of Derrida's discussion of intentionality. Indeed, intentionality, understood as the intention to signify something with the intermediary recourse to signs, represents for deconstruction the operator of the constitution of meaning. We should remember that the problematic of meaning is correlated to that of presence in the Derridean system: locutionary presence as intimate and unfailing presence of self-present subjectivity in speech.

Moreover, this theme forms one of the major critical anchoring points in Austin's theory and structures the quasi-totality of the dispute with Searle. In his critique of signification, Derrida remains a paradoxical Husserlian to the extent that deconstruction generalizes the primacy of voice as a manifestation of intentional presence in all the theories of signification it deconstructs. According to Derrida, signification rests on the hypostasis of speech, which is a linguistic modality determined primarily by an intended meaning applied to the signs of language in the act of enunciation. This conformation of the linguistic with the volitional is necessary for meaning to emerge. Conversely, the deconstructive approach ensures a description of the movement of the trace as the *exhaustion* of intentionality in writing. Indeed, the written text empties out the intentionality of the original thought and the intended meaning that is the source of its production: its textuality is shown to be ruled not by *will* [*vouloir*], but by *iteration*.[25]

Communication thus does not initiate the structurally iterative power of the written mark that conditions its legibility (to continue to lend itself to reading once the presence of the intention is dissipated) and its "citationality" (which allows one to take up a sequence of signs in a citation detached from its original context of production). However: "When I say 'my future disappearance,' I do so to make this proposition more immediately acceptable. I must be able simply to say my disappearance, my nonpresence in general, for example the nonpresence of my intended meaning, of my intention-to-signify, of my wanting-to-communicate-this, from the emission or production of the mark."[26] The vocabulary here is clearly phenomenological, revelatory of the way in which deconstruction systematically exposes the wheels of the phenomenological intentionality behind signification, representing the last avatar of voluntarism that dresses up Western metaphysics. If deconstruction is perfectly coherent as it applies to phenomenology, it is on the other hand more doubtful that it can be applied harmlessly to theories of meaning, primarily to Austin's theory, which has no connection to phenomenology.

We should recall the extent to which Derrida's arguments against Husserl remain fundamentally dependent on the latter's approach. The important point of reference here is Derrida's inaugural text published in 1967, *Voice and Phenomenon*, which was devoted to the Husserlian theory of signification. We see to what degree Husserl's intentionalist terminology influenced Derrida's elaboration of his deconstructive approach to metaphysics. As Derrida affirms in *Positions*:

I try to *write* (in) the space *in which is posed the question of speech and intended meaning*. I try to write the question: (what is) meaning to say? Therefore it is necessary in such a space, and guided by such a question, that writing literally mean nothing. Not that it is absurd in the way that absurdity has always been in solidarity with metaphysical meaning. It simply tempts itself, stretches itself, attempts to keep itself at the point of the breathlessness of intended meaning.[27]

Derrida proceeds by conceptual projection: metaphysics as a whole has merely been about what Husserl theorizes with regard to signification, such that metaphysics is founded on the evidence of the apophantic fecundity of *intended meaning* (in the subordination of the signs of language to the speaker's will to make meaning). Derrida conceives of phenomenological intentionality as the matrix of signification representing the epistemological motor of the unifying convergence of the will [*volonté*] to say something (the "intention to signify") and the signifiers of language.

Throughout, the Derridean method appears to remain dependent on the Husserlian phenomenological paradigm that it overturns and subverts but never truly escapes from, even in the critique of the possibility of expressive (and not indicative/indirect) communication, which it takes directly from Husserl's *Logical Investigations*. We see the ways in which the themes [*motifs*] are made and unmade: Derrida sees in communication the expression of an intended meaning at work, which Husserl had always denied, at least before *The Origin of Geometry*. Derrida plays Husserl against himself on this point and defends in turn an indexical, mediated, differing theory of communication against all other forms of communicational intentionalism.[28] If meaning is determined by the impression of the will in signs, once this will is detached from signs, these signs will return to the original state of semantic indetermination, of "dissemination" beneath or beyond volition. Presence thus represents only a moment in the life and destiny of signs, whose dissemination exceeds and exhausts its significance. The continuous legibility of signs is irreducible to the transient presence of the conveyed imprint of volition that characterizes the moment of utterance.

Thus living intention, that is, the meaning of the utterance, must be understood as a moment derived from the primordial and indeterminate legibility of the text. It is presence that results from the trace and not writing, whose task is to represent a supposedly originary presence. The value of the sign, which is dependent on "intended meaning," is only a moment in the greater process of semantic instability and indecision to which the sign is destined. Yet metaphysics lingers on this fragile moment, which is never continuous with the presence it hypostatizes. On the contrary, the deconstructive approach tends to show that the true significance of language lies above all else in a conception of the sign as *trace* or *deferral* of presence. Writing bears upon the workings of language such that intentional speech derives from textuality, and not the inverse. Thus the intended meaning of an utterance is revealed as forever incapable of being stabilized in the moment of communication, such that repeatable signs (in the act of rereading or rewriting) may activate new meanings by their iterative capacity. The repetition of signs, even those that are used in an intentionally determined utterance, *is always possible* and reveals the original detachment of signs vis-à-vis all intentional presence. The intentional presence never manages to coincide with, to latch itself onto, signs definitively. The precarious moment of utterance remains powerless to impose the hegemony of its animating will other than through the metaphysical illusion of a presence eternally continuous with itself and capable of surmounting the throes of writing. The sign itself, once used in a locutionary context, may be written, that is to say, repeated in another context in which it is no longer possible to capture the intention of its initial will to communicate.[29]

This theory of intended meaning particularly enriches the debate with Searle. This theory has already been the target of Derridean subversion: his description of writing, he warns us, will have as its consequence "the break with the horizon of the communication as the communication of consciousnesses or presences, and as the linguistic or semantic transport of meaning."[30] This critique is inscribed in a greater movement of deactivation of criteria of fixed meaning for signifying terms in their opening to "dissemination." It thus involves the deconstruction simultaneously of the semantic stability to which theories of communicational intention claim to raise language, as well as of any thesis that makes context a decisive instance in the determination of the meaning of utterance.[31] There remains the difficulty resulting from the fact that Derrida associates these two characteristics because he thinks that the contextualist theory itself is also founded on the primacy of intention, which is not at all clear (especially today when contemporary philosophy has seen the birth of Austinian representatives defending a contextualism detached from an absolute reference to intentionality).[32]

Derrida, as we will see, does not pay a great deal of attention to nonintentionalist theories of language and is himself an author who calls for a paradoxical conception of intentionality. He says very little about nonintentionalist theories of speech acts in the ensemble of texts of the debate that concerns us, with the exception of this especially illuminating remark, which reveals the theoretical distance that Derrida recognizes and accepts between deconstruction and a whole swath of analytic philosophy:

One might also reason that intention is not essential to speech acts or to anything else. Language, and many other things, would

then have to be questioned without making the intentional structure into a principle. In this case, to be sure, intention "doesn't
necessarily imply plenitude," and it lacks, even necessarily, qua
finite intention, plenitude. But that is not overly important and
one can treat this concept as a pragmatic concept (in the sense of
"empirically useful upon occasion, in such and such a context").
*This position would be shared by the nonintentionalisms and the empiricisms and
pragmatisms of different types. It is not mine.*[33]

WRITING AND CONTEXT(S)

Once these precautions are taken, a central question remains: what
real force to subvert contexts does Derrida attribute to writing?

The sign is detachable from the locutionary presence that sends it
at the present moment of the act of communication. This means that
the context of the communication's initial inscription (presence of
the sender, existence of a receiver) does not exhaust the capacities of
signs thus deployed to produce new meanings: the signs may repeat
themselves in circumstances that are no longer those of the initial act
of communication. The sign will find itself detached from its original
"intended meaning" and thus from the subjective will that animated
it contextually; it will continue to exist nonetheless graphically in the
form of a trace.

We may suppose that the signs mobilized here may be rewritten
without my knowledge, in which case they would emancipate themselves from the subjective control of my intention, which is to communicate certain information concerning Derrida's "SEC." Once
written elsewhere, they lose the intended meaning, which gave them

a defined semantic impetus: the signs will continue to exist, but my intention to signify something through them will have been lost due to this contextual displacement. In this scenario, the signs will have been detached from their *initial semantic content*. This detachment of signs through an ever-possible new usage comes to threaten the instant of communication since the dislocation of the unity of intention and signs proves likewise to be always possible. Such a possibility comes to haunt from within the fantasy of a fully realized unity of signifiers with the living intention of the speaker. It is only from a *semantic* point of view that signs appear empty, absurd in the transposition from one context to another, but deconstruction shows us that the semantic dimension is not fully aware of what a sign is, or that there exists *a purely graphic point of view* which considers the sign as a written trace and which, because uncoupled from its original intentional impetus, is reiterated indefinitely without an identifiable beginning or end to the process. Thus, since subjective presence ends up revealing itself as entirely secondary in relation to the iterative capacity of the sign, it becomes necessary to recognize an autonomy in the process of writing as differ*a*nce.[34] To do so, Derrida is driven to adopt increasingly technical metaphors (archive, duplicator, gramophone) that realize the infrasubjective movement of the trace. It is therefore necessary not to think of repetition as derived from presence, but rather to think of *presence as an effect of repetition*.

It is therefore necessary to distinguish between the *semantic* regime (the intentional investment of the sign) and the *graphic* regime (the persistent iteration of signs beyond intentional occurrences) in order to imagine the paradoxically transcendental primacy of the second regime over the first. This possibility of deferring [*différer*] the meaning of the sign through the written form of the sign, its rewriting or rereading detached from the intention of what one wants to say [*l'intention du vouloir-dire*], indicates thus the existence in the written sign of a "force of breaking with its context."[35] Two contextualist theses make up the object of the Derridean test: on the one hand, the "real" context; on the other, the "linguistic" context. The sign's "force of breaking" is applicable in the two scenarios. Here it is necessary to be especially careful with the lexicon Derrida employs to define what he understands by "context": "Are part of this alleged real context a certain 'present' of inscription, the presence of the scriptor in what he has written, the entire environment and horizon of his experience, and above all the intention, the meaning which at a given moment would animate his inscription."[36]

The definition of context given here prefigures the reading of Austin that Derrida will later offer, notably in the indifference to the failures of language that, according to Derrida, characterizes the author of *How to Do Things with Words*. Indeed, Derrida will produce a definition of context in terms retained from the primacy of the presence of consciousness. Context is here defined as the moment of the presence of the speaker at and in his speech, which implies a *considerable reduction* of context to *intentional presence* at the moment of inscription, at the present time of consciousness. We discover here an interpretive reflex of Husserlian technique where an "absolute" primacy is accorded to consciousness (in order to refute it at the next step). Context is thus here defined by Derrida as the exhaustive presence of the speaker at and in his enunciation. It is not at all clear that for Austin context is defined by "presence." On the contrary, Austin never ceased to submit intention to a world of conventions that precedes and conditions the deployment of speech acts: meaning in Austin is no longer conditioned by intention, but by the adequacy of words used to the circumstances required by conventions. Intention in Austin is inscribed in a global ensemble of circumstances greater than itself, over which it never possesses complete mastery, which explains why failure is an inherent possibility in every speech act. Starting with Austin, it is possible to make a distinction between *intention* and *speech act*: intention serves in the realization of the act, but does not have the transcendental role that Derrida, as an heir of Husserl, attributes to it: as the operator conditioning the pragmatic success of the performative act. The act may be accomplished even if my intention does not accompany it precisely because it is the *external circumstances and not the intentional* capacities that permit the realization of the speech act. I can, for example, want to christen a ship "Joseph Stalin" and be present intentionally at my utterance, which perfectly reflects my will, without my will accomplishing the act of christening because the circumstances were not favorable to the success of such an act.[37]

In Austin, the reality of the speech act is thus not solely dependent on my intention to effect it; *it requires circumstances propitious to its realization* (for example, am I the right person to christen the ship? do I have the authority to do so?). This distinction between the *intention* and the *act*, crucial in Austin, is possible only if the context is not reduced to intentional presence, as Derrida seems to assume is the case. This distinction is in reality only the effect of the root distinction between the constative and the performative that Austin accepts completely: for example, if I make a promise without the intention to make a promise, this does not in any way undermine the realization of the act of making a promise, which is not defective from the performative point of view since I promise *effectively* but *without sincerity*. What lends the reality of an act to the promise at its occurrence is not directly connected to its descriptive correspondence to a propositional attitude (turning the constative into a performative) that could be articulated thus: I never *wanted* to keep my promise so I never promised (the act was not accomplished). Austin radically critiques this schema of inference in the name of the underlying morality of his philosophy of ordinary language. In order to promise, it is sufficient for me to follow the standard procedure of the situation *whatever the degree of my interior adherence*. Indeed, Austin presents our *word* and not *our intentions* as our commitment ("Our word is our bond").[38] For this reason, Austin distinguishes between two types of infelicity in *HTW* and considers the absence of intention in the speech act not as a "misfire" but rather as a case of "abuse."[39] As regards the realization of the act, the case of infelicity in Austin belongs to conditions A and B; if these conditions are not fulfilled, the speech act does not take place. On the other hand, the absence of *intention* in the act belongs to the cases of infelicity distinguished by Austin as governed by the conditions Gamma, for which nonrespect undermines the *consistency* of the act (one would say in such a scenario the act is "empty") yet does not impede its realization. A promise made in insincerity, that is, without the intention of keeping it, is no less a promise. He who deals himself a promise cannot discard it, like Euripides's Hippolytus when he says, "my tongue swears the oath but not my heart,"[40] just because he did not intend to do so.[41] It will thus not be said that this promise has not taken place, but rather that it was poorly made, which is no way releases its holder of responsibility: on the contrary, since "our word is our bond," the grammar of the promise *commits* the one who makes it to the person who receives it, whether or not the former is sincere.[42] The intention for Austin has significance since it renders it a "false promise," but this falsity does not belong to the *act* of promising, which itself is very real. It is only false in the sense that it will deceive the person to whom it was made: it is a case of abuse.

To return to "SEC," Derrida affirms that the true force of rupture with the logic of intention thus does not lie in the distinction between intention and act, *but between intention and the written sign*, in that "by all rights, it belongs to the sign to be legible, even if the moment of its production is irremediably lost, and even if I do not know what its alleged author-scriptor meant consciously and intentionally at the moment he wrote it, that is abandoned it to its essential drifting."[43] In other words, one may read a text detached from the context in which it was sent, that is, without managing to reattach it to its original intention, to the established intention that produced it. Thus written inscription indicates an *undecidability* for the meaning of the sequence of signs retranscribed in a context different from the first intentional context. The primordial status of such undecidability with regard to signification allows Derrida to deconstruct the myth of a pragmatic convergence of interlocutors in communication.

Another context addressed by Derrida: as far as the "the semiotic . . . context" is concerned, "there is no less a force of breaking,"[44] given that the written sign has the same capacity for detachment from its propositional context. For Derrida, against Hegel, the moment of the negative is not recoverable in a "sublimation" that would assure the integration of the graphic trace in the totalizing process of self-presence: the force of rupture in the negativity of the written trace makes it reluctant to participate fully in the intentional process of signification (of the becoming of *meaning* from the *sign* effected by its intentional investment).[45] According to Derrida, the relation between the present intention and the sign remains marked by an insurmountable heterogeneity. The text is characterized as much by its meaning as by the series of "spacings" between the written signs it produces. Necessary to any genuine consideration of textuality, these spacings attest to the individual independence of the signifying elements that compose the text and finish by destroying from within the contextual holism of meaning—where all elements depend on one another—in the production of insoluble semantic distances: "This spacing is not the simple negativity of a lack, but the emergence of the mark. However, it is not the work of the negative in the service of meaning, or of the living concept, the *telos*, which remains *relevable* and reducible in the *Aufhebung* of a dialectics."[46]

The splintering of the component parts of the proposition represents this second consequence of the *contextual rupture* provoked by the trace. Thus writing does not represent a case apart, a rupture with the paradigm of communication, but rather the rupture internal to all communication in general. Writing becomes the unexpected model from which to think the limits of all recourse to language, "marked" from within by the unsuspected effects of absence inherent in speech. Derrida also invites us to consider "any element of spoken language,"[47] the way its function depends on a code and defines its pertinent field of use in order to make meaning; its grammatical identity depends on this normative codification.

This codification is what allows us to distinguish a mark from a sign, a conjunction from a noun or a verb, in that each element is correlated to a determined grammatical function that permits its reiteration. For example, a noun is repeated as a noun from one sentence to another; its grammatical identity remains unmodified in repetition. Since his thesis, however, is that the process of writing is the rule of language, just as it is its most intimate and hidden mode of dysfunction, Derrida asks: "Why is this identity paradoxically the division or dissociation from itself which will make of this phonic sign a grapheme?"[48]

Here Derrida affirms that the phonic sign masks a deeper graphic nonidentity, and that therefore the self-identity of the signifier and the place it invariably occupies in a propositional structure are factitious, since its identity depends on its iteration; a noun is not a noun unless it remains a noun, unless its iteration stabilizes it. Iteration, however, is a double-edged concept: it demonstrates the grammatical stability assigned to logical occurrence as well as its profound instability, provoked by the condemnation of identity never to exist except in self-repetition, provoking its inevitable identification with its own reduplication, with a self indefinitely differed in its other. Self-identity is broken once it requires repetition to affirm and confirm its positivity; we enter into a scenario of infinite regression in which self-affirmation affirms only the duty to affirm oneself through repetition, such that repetition reveals the ways it conditions identity, rather than the inverse. Repetition is shown as a process that simultaneously conditions and splits self-identity, such that "the presence of the present is thought beginning from the fold of the return, beginning from the movement of repetition and not the reverse."[49] Repetition is no longer conditioned by a prior ideal form it repeats. The form itself is a product of repetition since it paradoxically draws its own ideal positivity from repetition. Conditioned by what it claims to condition, repetition is also as essential to the essential form as form is to repetition, of which it is now only the effect. Repetition is thus revealed to be more original than the identity of origin that rationally conditions repetition as repetition of the Same. The Same thus emanates from the illusory fixation of a more profound dynamic—differance—that engenders and deconstructs it *at the same time*. The affirmation of self takes as its condition the repetition of this affirmation; an affirmation that must be repeated in order to affirm itself no longer affirms anything but its own inability to affirm.[50]

In repetition the graphic trace is cut from the productive presence of meaning; it is diffused beyond the generative subjective presence of meaning. Signification is thus paralyzed to the extent it clashes with the iterative subversion of the graphic trace, as the "remaindrance,"[51] irreducible to the volitional presence of the subject who seeks to animate it fully in the intention of signification.[52] The trace is deployed iteratively, independently of the presence of all signifieds and referents. Derrida attributes the discovery of the fact that language may do without any ideal (signified) or real (referent) correlates to the advances made by Husserl in *Logical Investigations*.

FROM INTENTIONALITY TO CITATIONALITY

Derrida retains four fundamental points of the Husserlian analysis developed in *Logical Investigations* in order to advance his own theory of the written mark:

(1) A utterance [*énoncé*] never needs its referent to be "present" to the perception either of the speaker or of the interlocutor in order to

have an intelligible meaning. It is sufficient for the discourse to refer to a possible signified object. Thus the absence of "intuitive fulfillment" of the sign's aim never calls into question the logical consistency of the utterance produced. Indeed, the aim of the sign is to set its sights on the possible object via the signified; the sign intends the object on the horizon of a *possible* referential confirmation (the confirmation of the presence of the object in this world). The absence of the object sought is thus not detrimental to either meaning or communication: "If I say, while looking out the window, 'The sky is blue,' the statement will be intelligible (let us provisionally say, if you will, communicable), even if the interlocutor does not see the sky; even if I do not see it myself, if I see it poorly, if I am mistaken, or if I wish to trick my interlocutor. Not that it is always thus; but the structure of possibility of this statement includes the capability of being formed and of functioning either as an empty reference, or cut off from its referent."[53]

(2) There exists a functional modality for the autonomous sign in relation to its attachment to a signified: the "crisis" of the sciences described by Husserl rests on the reduction of the sign to a pure operability detached from all ties to signification: the scientist's activity is reduced to the manipulation of symbols cut off from their original intentional source: "I can manipulate symbols without an active and current fashion animating them with my attention and intention to signify (the crisis of mathematical symbolism, according to Husserl)."[54] The absence of the signified, however, never short-circuits the efficacious utilization of the sign since "Husserl indeed stresses the fact that this does not prevent the sign from functioning: the crisis or vacuity of mathematical meaning does not limit techni-cal progress."[55] If one refers to the first works of Derrida on Husserl,

one notices that his own theory has always greatly amplified Husserl's assessment of the scope of the crisis of the sign engendered by the mathematization of nature, through which systems of signs will prove capable of functioning independently of the reactivated presence of the meanings originally constituted in the world of life.

(3) On the other hand, Husserl accepts nonobjective significations (that do not have as their function to aim for present or possible objects), such as the proposition "the circle is square," which is "a proposition invested with meaning. It has enough meaning for me to be able to judge it false or contradictory."[56] Here Derrida leans on the Husserlian distinction between *widersinnig* and *sinnlos* (between contradiction and meaninglessness). Contradiction, the impossible correlation between an utterance and an object, can only be identified if meaning remains inassimilable to objective signification. If meaning was reduced to objective signification, contradictory utterances could never make sense for us as contradictions. Thus "'square circle' marks the absence of a referent, certainly, and also the absence of a certain signified, but not the absence of meaning."[57] Derrida considers writing, defined as an economy of rupture with the sign's intentional presence (leading from sign to signified) and intuitive presence (leading from signification to reference), as the pathogenic element responsible for such possibilities of phenomenological uncoupling between the sign and the signified or the referential presence.

(4) On the other hand, in the case of *Sinnlosigkeit*, language, by its agrammaticality, loses all hold on meaning: the examples from Husserl taken up by Derrida are "green is or" and "abracadabra." In the preceding cases (1, 2, and 3), Derrida tells us, the propositions were

detached from their signification *but never from a logical structure teleo-logically determined* by access to signifieds or to objects given in person through intuition. The contract of meaning was certainly not fulfilled in the preceding cases, but only through "deception," "crisis," or contradiction, and not through a *structural* incapacity.

In the last case (4), by contrast, it is the absence of grammatical coherence that paralyzes every vague intention, in which case there is certainly no longer any meaning, but also no longer any *possibility of making meaning*. We are faced here precisely with the case of pure graphic design, in other words, with a sequence of signs that can no longer answer for meaning. Contrary to the first examples, which were dependent on the teleological horizon of meaning, "the green is or" refers to the "absolute of absence" that I have previously evoked. The utterance "the green is or" demonstrates a form of *radical* absence of meaning. As Derrida reminds us, the specificity of *Logical Investigations*, particularly the fourth investigation, rests upon the foundation of a universal logical grammar that describes the a priori conditions thanks to which a proposition may enter into a relation of possible knowledge with an object. The approach to language that describes pure grammatical structures fuses with the exclusive problematic of truth. Thus language in Husserl can only be approached from the logocentric horizon of the apophantic.[58] The preceding cases of an absence of referent and signified do not depart from this opening axiom since, for example, the status of the utterance "the circle is square" depends on the question of truth as the operator determining its logical status (here contradictory).

The case of "the green is or" is more complex since this type of utterance escapes the hold of logic and situates itself subversively in the margins of all structural possibility of signifying anything. This is why this utterance is more paradigmatic than the others in emphasizing the devastating effects of writing; it allows one to conceive the hiatus that maintains a distance between the utterance and the intentional context that originally produced its meaning. Detached from every "horizon of truth," unresponsive to the "universal conditions of possibility for a morphology of significations in the relation of knowledge to a possible object,"[59] the utterance "the green is or" demonstrates in an exemplary fashion the capacity of language to liberate itself from its metaphysical dependence on the problematic of truth, and to expose thus its capacity for *radical rupture* with the register of presence. This utterance reveals the contextual wandering par excellence of language as writing, and even announces thereby the end of its metaphysical raison d'être (conditioned by signification, truth, and intention). Context, for Derrida, is assimilated at the moment of the intentional production of the utterance, but here the uncoupling of language from the logic of intended meaning condemns a priori all possibility of reattaching a sequence of signs to a context of stabilized production in univocal fashion.

Despite an absence of signification, the utterance "the green is or" is exemplary of the movement of the written mark insofar as it allows us to understand that the relation between the utterance and its context is ordered not by the logic of the intended meaning, but by the artificiality of the *graft*. We understand "the green is or" because the meaning is the systematic result not of the original and productive intention, but of a *graft* by which the utterance appears to resist any determined intentional assignment: every sequence of signs may be articulated *at the same time* for divergent contexts of utterance.

The same utterance, "the green is or," as a layout of marks, and as a mark itself, possesses neither an apophantic topos nor a logical fate to fulfill a priori; it begins to make meaning insofar as, by definition, no meaning is ever compelled a priori. *The utterance begins to make meaning by derivation* from its previous graphic structure. A sequence of signs functions semantically in a context because it is previously grafted on it, indicating that its meaning could not depend on its belonging *exclusively* to a determined context. Indeed, the grafted phrase belongs only artificially to the context into which it is carried; its power of detachment in the context is contemporaneous with its temporary imbrication with the context. As a consequence every performative utterance that is present, which is to say, inscribed in a determined context, *always* belongs to an indefinite multiplicity of other contexts *at the same time*. The performative power of the sequence of signs mobilized in the present systematically escapes the intention that mobilizes it in a contextualized performative act. The sequence "the green is or" belongs *simultaneously* to three different contexts that cannot be ordered hierarchically since the criteria for the appropriateness of an utterance to its context (taking as its crux the intentional presence that produces meaning) are no longer valid. If there is no privileged context, "the green is or" [*le vert est ou*] can at least be related to three intentional contexts at the same time without reducing itself to any of them, since it, always grafted, may be endlessly grafted onto other contexts. The sequence "the green is where" [*le vert est où*] may be grafted onto extremely diverse contexts: I can mean to say, "the glass is where" [*le verre est où*], as in, "Where did the glass go?" [*Où est passé le verre?*], but the grafted nature of my utterance indicates that I may also say, without meaning to, "the green is where" and be speaking of a lawn, the "or" [*ou*] in the two preceding cases becoming "where" [*où*] to the listener; but this utterance can also mean "the green is or," *an example of ungrammaticality.* An utterance is thus never saturated by a context of production; it has no center of privileged expressive emanation. Its meaning remains for this reason finally *undecidable.* The point of view adopted here is no longer that of the articulation of words according to their intentional invest-ment (which would settle the meaning) but of the words themselves that, independently of intentional presence, remain resistant to all stabilized contextual anchoring. To deconstruct means to expose the dissident "legality" of the sign in relation to the logic of presence, a "legality" that takes as its form the nonregulated destabilization of all apophantic legality through the infinite iteration of signs, always already grafted in advance onto an overflow of contexts that escape the attention of the speaker using them. The present context does not saturate the graphic disposition of a sequence of signs capable of being grafted onto an indefinite series of contexts latent to it, that is to say, capable of continuing to make meaning, to perform, *beyond all determined intentional mobilization.* In this way, an utterance may be pulled from its place of origin, from the original intention that governs it, in order to be grafted onto new contexts of production, without it being somehow possible to contain or master such a movement: "This is the possibility on which I wish to insist: the possibility of extraction and of citational grafting which belongs to the structure of every mark, spoken or written, and which constitutes every mark as writing even before and outside every horizon of semiolinguistic communication; as writing, that is, as a possibility of functioning cut off, at a certain point, from its 'original' meaning and from its belonging to a saturable and constraining context."[60] A sequence of uttered signs is thus characterized by its capacity to be *cited*, that is to say, extracted from its original context in order to perform in contexts that were not originally its own, the deployment of the written mark having rendered null and void the opposition between the proper and improper.

The generalized displacement of produced utterances reveals the fact that utterance is not antecedent to citation; on the contrary, all discourse is always already *cited* in advance. The issue is thus for Derrida to awaken the latent contexts that all utterances carry with them despite themselves. Here the context is no longer defined exclusively according to the category of presence since presence indicates a hierarchy of contexts relative to the present intention. On the contrary, for the deconstructive system the point is to accept the mixing of contexts through which an utterance continues *to mean to say* independently of and beyond its present signification, without end. In other words, there exists a multiplicity of intentions contemporaneous with that to which the speaker submits, in the present moment, the signs that he mobilizes. The trace detached from its productive origin sees itself above all as exportable and capable of migrating without limit toward new contexts. The field of contextual renewal is in sum infinite since all contexts are likely to cite portions of signs. As a written mark, the sign endlessly engenders new contexts of insertion for the performative utterance.

AUSTIN: DISCIPLE OF NIETZSCHE?

Derrida considers Austin a thinker of communication in his analyses of illocutionary as well as perlocutionary acts: "Austin, by his emphasis on the analysis of perlocution and especially illocution, indeed seems to consider acts of discourse only as acts of communication."[61] Yet there is a great difference between *ordering* X to do Y (Austin's position on illocutionary value) and communicating to X the fact that he is ordered to do Y (the position of those who adhere to communicational pragmatism: Grice and Searle on the illocutionary).[62] In the first case the use of language is entirely performative, in the other the modality of the acts remains from beginning to end descriptive/constative since the speaker is simply transmitting to X a will to be obeyed and to see Y accomplished. But when I address X, do I order him, that is, *do I do something* with my words, or do I transmit to him my intention to see him obey? Here the distinction between constative and performative is at play, for in the second case I do not order, but rather I transmit an intention to see X obey and I wait for him to understand, which means that Austin's communicational interpretation destroys the performative modality of language. By ordering, one no longer *does* anything, one is satisfied with *transmitting the presence of an intention*, reducing a speech act to the transmission of a propositional attitude for the interlocutor to understand: this places the illocutionary force on the descriptive/constative terrain, and no longer on the terrain of performative accomplishment as Austin wishes. It is hard to see how a communicational interpretation of speech acts allows one to respect the intelligibility of such a transition. Furthermore, Derrida's connection of Austin with Nietzsche with regard to the communication of an illocutionary or perlocutionary "force" adds a supplementary misunderstanding between Derrida and Austin. How does Derrida create such a connection and what does this connection teach us about the distortion to which Derrida submits Austin? The crucial problem of the Derridean analysis remains the *naturalization* of the illocutionary force in the "will to power" and its reduction to a perlocutionary phenomenon. This confusion rests on the persistent idea in Derrida that illocutionary acts are *communicated* (I communicate a "force" through the performative act). Derrida considers the Austinian transition from "meaning" to "force" properly Nietzschean. It is clear that this connection is seductive, and in one sense not false; however, it does not illuminate Austin's point.

It is true that Austin speaks of "illocutionary force" in order to account for a linguistic dimension that is no longer *descriptive* but *active* in practice. This is moreover the main argument of *HTW*: the clearing of a zone of investigation in language largely ignored by logical positivism, which had centered its theoretical preoccupations on the assertive value of utterances. By focusing his attention on ordinary uses of language, Austin sought to substitute the values of "act," "force," and "felicity" for the values of "meaning" and "truth." What interests Derrida is this performative dimension in Austin, which allows us to see uses of language detached from all dependence on metaphysical truth. Such a theory allows a break with the "logocentric" axioms that Derrida seeks to deconstruct. But if the deconstruction of the logocentrism of assertion connects Austin and Derrida, as Stanley Cavell has emphasized,[63] it is nonetheless not at all certain that the line of convergence passes through Nietzsche, as Derrida thinks: "Austin had to free the analysis of the performative from the authority of the *value of truth*, from the opposition true/false, at least in its classical form, occasionally substituting for it the value of force, of difference of force (*illocutionary or perlocutionary force*). (It is this, in a thought which is nothing less than Nietzschean, which seems to me to beckon towards Nietzsche; who often recognized in himself a certain affinity with a vein of English thought.)"[64] The first part of the analysis appears incontestable; Austin clearly abandons the attempt to see the functioning of language from the point of view of the "truth/falsehood fetish." However, the second part of the analysis appears largely contestable, a source of all the misunderstandings in the continental reception of Austin. If this deconstructive reappropriation of Austin has something laudable about it, it nonetheless creates distortions that Austinian theory was no doubt unprepared for.

Why does it seem to us detrimental to invoke Nietzsche in order to explain Austin?

It is necessary here to ask how deconstruction uses Nietzsche generally. For the very movement by which deconstruction is staged [*se met en scène*] relies on authors who, one by one in Derrida's readings, each illuminate a new aspect of differance. Nietzsche is invoked early on by Derrida, starting in *Writing and Difference* in 1973. In the essay entitled "Structure, Sign, and Play in the Discourse of the Human Sciences," the figure of Nietzsche appears at a point in the argument nearly equivalent to the one that concerns us here, on the overcoming—which the reference to Nietzsche allows—of the teleological perspective of language in the liberation of the forces of becoming, which lack any metaphysical center of gravity.[65] But we should not forget the preceding page of "SEC," where Derrida, thanks to Husserl, finally discovered the true citational determination of signs. This discovery was made possible in the argumentation because of the fact that the utterance "the green is or" was revealed as radically marking the distance in relation to all teleological contexts in which assertion remained the exclusive horizon of language. Thus "the green is or" became exportable, liberated from one context and another solely because of its lack of reason, its disseminal absence of teleological determination.[66]

It is undeniable that Austin relativizes the primacy of assertion; on the other hand, it is not at all certain that an alternative exists for Austin, either in Nietzsche or even in the nonlogical profusion of forces that Derrida finds there (ensuring the transition from signification as the production of intended meaning to blows of force as the will liberated from all rational fate).

There are several reasons for this, but first let us articulate Stanley Cavell's argument, which questions the relevance of the connection between Austin and Nietzsche proposed by Derrida. According to Cavell, it is clear that the question of truth/falsehood does not apply to the performative; on the other hand, it is deceptive to make Austin Nietzschean to the extent that he *proposes new criteria for agreement between language and the world*, no longer passing through the descriptivist system of correspondences but through *conventions* and *uses*. Thus the properly conventional approach to the performative allows for the emergence of a new conception of truth that no longer owes anything to that of logocentric positivism, but that has *no relation* to the deconstruction of logic as Nietzsche and, after him, Derrida propose.[67] Cavell's commentary emphasizes the fact that Austin does not seek to deconstruct the value of truth (as the adequacy of language to that which is) as much as to shift the focus of this question to the meaning that it acquires when measured against the problematic of ordinary performatives. One cannot deny that

Austin seeks to relativize the primacy of assertion in favor of a broader account of the potentialities of language. As such, it is true, as Derrida emphasizes, that the performative "does not describe something which exists outside and before language. It produces or transforms a situation, it operates."[68] However, the reversal of logocentrism does not necessarily indicate the transition from meaning (as adequacy of language to presence) to the will liberated from all logic, as the reference to Nietzsche suggests. As I emphasized earlier, there is in Derrida a dichotomous apprehension of language that forbids the emergence of a *new conception of the rationality of language*, a conception indifferent to the metaphysical problem of truth and that, by its very indifference, allows us to think of a *nonapophantic logic* at work in ordinary practices. The Austinian gesture consists in making a renewed apprehension of language possible, starting from a logic that does not owe any allegiance to the metaphysical problematic of truth. Austin's illocutionary "force" rests on *perfectly rational* conventional mechanisms, whose logic, however, remains at the same time irreducible *both* to the logocentrism of truth *and* to the arbitrary deployment of a force with incalculable effects emanating from the will, a force that Derrida's reference to Nietzsche seems to pose as the *only* alternative to logocentrism. Austin's theory does not consider the illocutionary force as the *emanation of a will*. The illocutionary "force" does not originate in the natural effects of language produced by the *will* on others, but in the conformity to convention that *alone* lends utterance its performative impact. The illocutionary force of an utterance depends on its conformity to a ritual ordered by convention, for which it is necessary that the circumstances *external to the will* be reunited (for example, in a hierarchy, that I rank as superior to someone in order *to succeed* in giving him an order). Moreover, and most importantly, the force of the illocutionary act *is conventional*, that is, the act indicates a certain number of effects *defined by convention* (for example, a promise commits me to someone). This *efficacy of pragmatic force* has nothing natural about it; it is tied to the artificiality of rules that define the uses of language. But if Derrida is right to point to the originality of Austinian displacement (the transition from "meaning" to "force"), he does not do justice to the nuance between the two types of "force" distinguished by Austin (on the one hand the illocutionary "force" of *conventional* effects, on the other the perlocutionary "force" whose effects are *natural*); in a highly contestable gesture, he combines them in order to deconstruct them more easily, as if they both belonged to a metaphysics of intention. If one had to connect Austin and Nietzsche, it would be through the second category of acts, but this connection would carry too heavy a price: the lack of distinction between the two types of force would produce an assimilating dissolution of the illocutionary in the perlocutionary. This will constitute, as we will see, a central argument in Searle's critique of the Derridean reading of Austin. What fascinates Derrida in Nietzsche, what he despairs of not finding in Austin, is the thematic *of an intention that is unpredictable in its effects*.

This fragility may indeed be found in Austin on the side of the perlocutionary, since the perlocutionary, if rooted in an intention, is experienced in a natural exteriority that carries the act beyond itself without the result of the intention being *predictable* beforehand: I can have the intention to insult another without knowing if my act will have the *desired effect* on him. More than the illocutionary, the perlocutionary indeed depends on a *cognitive nonmastery* of consciousness over the act that occurs on the terrain of natural effectiveness, through effects on another person that the act may or may not produce. Derrida thus reproaches Austin for not having gone far enough in the analysis of a force that cannot be cognitively mastered, and for thereby revalorizing a teleological intentionality in the illocutionary act. This reproach would be justified if Austin had reduced his theory *to perlocutionary acts alone* and in such a scenario had proposed to ground the perlocutionary teleologically—which would have contradicted Austin's own theory of perlocutionary "force." But this is not absolutely the case since Austin, above all else, describes cognition's ascendancy over the perlocutionary as impossible, and at the same time poses as a condition of success for the illocutionary act not its conformation to a *cognitive will* (an intention imposing a teleological meaning on mobilized signs), but its *conformity* to a conventional procedure that may be realized in appropriate circumstances. Therein resides the specificity of the illocutionary force, for which the source of impact and efficacy is precisely not the will (intentional/teleological or not [as "will to power"]).

It is thus impossible to make the Austinian performative into a concept that insidiously reproduces the problematic of intentional presence, and to consider it a disguised logocentric constative. Derrida's reversal relies on coordinates that are highly contestable from the Austinian point of view: to the autonomous will that imposes on the signs it deploys their entire pragmatic value, without remainder, Derrida opposes a force, a will to power whose expression escapes all rational mastery of the effects it produces. But if the promise involves causal necessity (the activity of promising having the effect of committing the one who promises, for example), this necessity does not have its source in the subjective presence that imposes a certain logical or pragmatic fate on signs (in Husserl their conformity to a signified or a reference; here their conformity to a logico-pragmatic framework decided in the upper reaches of the intention); the force of the promise depends on the regulation of conventions alone. When I speak, I do not therefore exercise *my own power* or natural force, but rather the power of the conventional definition of the promise on which the effects it engenders are necessarily dependent, which remains perfectly indifferent to what I *would like* it to be or not to be (such moreover is the meaning of Austin's reference to *Hippolytus*). In order to subvert the Austinian performative, Derrida will propose to upset the presumed relation between the will and the written mark by passing from the predictable to the unpredictable in speech acts. This reversal only makes sense if one conceptualizes the functioning of illocutionary force on the model of perlocutionary force. For Derrida, the good performative is a well-executed Austinian perlocutionary, that is, an act invested by an intention from which it effectively draws its force, but whose impact remains unpredictable (since I am never assured of the success of my act, success depending *precisely not on my intention* in the case of the perlocutionary). But such a Derridean performative is only possible on the basis of a denial about the specificity of illocutionary efficacy described by Austin.

Without returning directly to Nietzsche's terminology, Derrida will later propose a reversal of this order in his elaboration of the promise. Here Derrida wants to expose a performative that no longer owes anything to the supposed intentional mastery of the Austinian illocutionary; he does this through the test of the *impossible* that every promise involves. Liberated from all teleology, the act of promising releases, in opposition to any calculation, an unpredictable *future to come* [*à-venir*] for the intentional consciousness whose efficacy exceeds its capacity for anticipation.[69] But this subversion of the performative, moving from calculation to the unpredictable, makes sense only in the frame of a reversed neophenomenological approach that establishes consciousnesses as the command center for the illocutionary impact of speech acts, which Austin absolutely does not do. Decentering the performative from the conscious, calculated mastery of its effects does not mean anything to Austin, for whom the illocutionary remains predictable in its effects, but certainly not because consciousness determines teleologically the act to have any particular illocutionary effect. The powerlessness of intention before the *conventionally regulated* effects of the illocutionary indicates that the question of unpredictability and its stakes can only be posed for the perlocutionary, for which the Nietzschean-Derridean play of forces will finally be applicable.

From the Austinian point of view, the flaw in this approach rests on the restrictive alternative that it proposes: leaving the choice solely between a teleological intentionality of meaning (which is for Derrida the principle on which the functioning of the performative rests in Austin) and an ateleological act (freed from presence in the test of the *unpredictable* created by the act of promising). We see here a tension—internal to Derrida's thought—between two towering figures of continental thought, Husserl and Nietzsche, that has no real relation to the originality of Austin's analyses, which concern the success of the performative that does not depend on will alone, teleological or not.

AUSTIN: INTENTIONALIST AUTHOR?

Despite the reversal that Austin performs in the transition from "meaning" to "force," he has not, Derrida affirms, "taken into account that which in the structure of *locution* (and therefore before any illocutionary or perlocutionary determination) already bears within itself the system of predicates that I call *graphematic in general*, which therefore confuses all the ulterior oppositions whose pertinence, purity, and rigor Austin sought to establish in vain."[70]

Here Austin is accused of rehabilitating the oppositional structure of the metaphysics of presence. To this metaphysics Derrida opposes "the system of graphematic predicates" that initiates every locution (all sensible speech) before it is assigned to a pragmatic task (illocutionary or perlocutionary). By refusing to take such graphematic predicates into account, Austin reproduces the most classic theoretical conclusions of the metaphysics of presence. The first cause of this rehabilitation of presence rests on Austin's unreserved adherence to a notion of *context*. Derrida criticizes the existence in Austin's philosophy of a criterion of demarcation that allows one to distinguish between a successful or failed performative. This division is indeed teleologically directed by the value of a context whose logic derives from the values of the metaphysical conformity of language to the truth, which Austin's destabilization of the truth/falsehood fetish should have, to remain coherent, rendered void. For according to Derrida, the total context *requires a locutionary presence conscious of itself, its performative aim, and the means by which it may accomplish it.* Derrida sees in Austin the construction of a new fetish in the transition from the "value of truth" to the "value of context."[71] Context may be clearly determined from a certain number of criteria and becomes the value to which the utterance must conform in order to obtain pragmatic value. To use Austin's example, when the procedure is not "accepted"[72] by convention, the act is considered void; thus in divorce procedures ("We're divorced now!") that do not take place in an adequate context accepted by convention, the act is null and void according to rule A.2 outlined by Austin: "The particular persons and circumstances in a given case must be appropriate for the invocation for the particular procedure involved."[73] The act is valid only if the circumstances required for the fulfillment of the performative are unified. But Derrida tells us that if the elements that "might affect the event of the performative" are revealed faulty at the moment of the fulfillment of the act, there is "the conscious presence of the intention of the speaking subject for the totality of his locutory act. Thereby, performative communication once more becomes the communication of an intentional meaning, even if this meaning has no referent in the form of a prior or exterior thing or state of things."[74] Derrida sees in Austin the principle of metaphysical presence rehabilitated: the contextual presence, or the presence of the speaking subject of illocutionary or perlocutionary *meaning* produced by his intentions. The question that Derrida asks about Austin's doctrine could be formulated thus: does this theory put an end to the privilege of speech, to the fantasy of total mastery and fully synthetic adherence to the words of our intentions?

Austin is accused of setting the play of signifiers to the rhythm of the pulse of living consciousness, alone capable of rendering them spiritually dynamic and of opening them thus to an ideality of meaning for which pragmatic value would only be another sly avatar. Although Derrida acknowledges Austin's evacuation of standard referential terms ("thing" or "state of things"), the performative still represents a mere modification of a most intentional, most metaphysical concept of "meaning." Here it is interesting to note that, in believing he is deconstructing Austin's theory, Derrida, in an increasingly involuntary way, is already aiming at Searle's theory, whose characteristics include the attempt to rethink the performative through intentionality.

On the other hand, Austin remains an author whose approach distances itself radically from the subjectivism that Derrida projects onto him. In the end, Derrida wants to lead Austin back to a subjectivist thesis.

THE PROBLEM OF CITATIONALITY IN AUSTIN

The reformulation of canonical oppositions in metaphysics, principally the opposition between essence and accident, finds its translation in Austin's exclusion of infelicities. Infelicity is treated as an event that does not affect the interior of the speech act, as an incident that supervenes from the exterior and has no power to alter its deeper structure. For Austin, infelicities are redirected and thus even reduced to the status of contingent factors. Austin, however, is obliged to recognize that infelicities represent a possibility inherent in all conventional acts, which are inevitably exposed to them. There remains the question of knowing whether this exposure *is or is not constitutive*. According to Derrida, Austin inclines toward the first hypothesis, believing himself able to free the purified structure of the speech act, isolating it thus to abstract it from the contingency of infelicity. Thus, when even the possibility of infelicity remains irreducible because no speech act could take place without exposure to infelicity, Austin maintains that infelicity does not have the least effect on the essence of the act, which, for its part, could be freed and described by theory in its most intact purity. For this idea to stand, it is necessary to presuppose the existence of a dimension of a purely ideal analysis of the act, this presupposition having in effect as its corollary the exclusion of infelicity, which indeed no longer teaches us anything about the linguistic phenomenon under consideration. The theoretical consequence of the reactivation of the metaphysical essence/accident distinction in Austin echoes, second, in the "second gesture of exclusion"[75] involving citations—these being considered by Austin as parasitic uses of language—*deviant* cases in relation to *ordinary uses*. The concept of "ordinary language" presupposes a hierarchy of uses of language, some more normal than others, and as such slyly reactivates the principles of a properly metaphysical axiology.[76] Austin excludes *cited* utterances from his theory. These are not considered in his theory since they represent a use that is merely *parasitic* to the ordinary or "normal" use. Derrida reminds us, however: "It is also as a 'parasite' that writing has always been treated by the philosophical tradition, and the rapprochement, here, is not at all fortuitous."[77] A citation, a sequence of signs radically cut off from its locutionary origin, represents, like writing, a figure of differance in the Derridean economy. One thus finds in Austin this same metaphysical gesture of repression of the *deferred* [*différé*]—like an unintended return of the utterance in citation—in the same court of judgment as writing: as a deviant phenomenon to be excluded. A theoretical norm may be established on the basis of this exclusion by modeling its descriptive injunctions and prescriptions on the universal pedestal of present temporality, for which the concept of "ordinary language" represents only a deceptive avatar. The question asked by Derrida could be formulated thus: is this possibility of the parasite, of the deformation of normal usage, *internal and constitutive* of the usage said to be normal or *external and accidental*? For philosophy in general, writing is conceived as an exterior threat to logos, powerless to affect the interior of speech inscribed in the horizon of truth as presence. The deconstructive thesis takes the reverse of this conception: original presence *deferred* in writing is not external to the logocentrized philosophical system; *différance is internal to it* as an intimate possibility that contaminates it from within. In this way, speech becomes an effect of writing in the sense that these two terms are no longer opposed, but imply each other reciprocally as the two sides of the generalized movement of *différance*. This is why normal usage in Derrida always depends on the parasite as its paradoxical condition of possibility, from which it draws its discriminating power, its normative and regulating force. Exclusion functions like the founding act of normative affirmation; it is thus revealed as not only exterior to the purity of the phenomenon considered, *but also* constitutive of a moment of its determination and its disavowed and nonetheless inevitable ontological concession to the other that it excludes, at the very moment of this exclusion. Parasitism is paradoxically shown as constitutive of the norm, internal to all positivity of meaning.

For this reason, infelicity could not represent a contingent incident on the path of some pure and adequate progression of the performative. Because it is unavoidable (an act can always fail, being contaminated in advance by this eventuality before one can isolate it ideally), infelicity is *a possibility constitutive of the act*.[78] The exclusion of citations becomes the exclusion of the generalized graphematic by which every performative event is *always already cited*. If every performative is cited in advance, however, it becomes necessary to recognize that the successful performative is derivative of the citation, which functions as the condition of possibility of all performative acts.[79] Indeed, a performative utterance [*énoncé*] depends on a convention, that is, on a normative code by which it is validated, this code being defined by its iterability (in baptisms, for example, only the same procedure that repeats a conventional procedure is accepted). The uniqueness of the event of performative felicity depends on a *prior and constitutive iterability* of conventions to which the performative confirms by repeating the model, itself iterable, of the generic procedure that allows for its accomplishment: "Could a performative statement succeed if its formation did not repeat a 'coded' or iterable statement, in other words if the expressions I use to open a meeting, launch a ship or a marriage were not identifiable as *conforming* to an iterable model, and therefore if they were not identifiable in a way as 'citation'?"[80] Thus, the *present* speech act is only possible if it *repeats* an adequate procedure that necessarily precedes it and that is defined by its iterability.

Therefore the public officer who makes a marriage official with the performative formula "I declare you man and wife" is only submitting to highly precise and rehearsed rules; he is exactly like an actor on the stage *reciting* his text. The performative text ("I declare you man and wife," "I baptize this child," and the like) always precedes its use, and in this respect, the text must always be recognized as that which precedes and conditions presence. In ordinary life we are all like actors repeating a textual script such that it becomes impossible to inaugurate performative usages more "serious" than others.

SIGNING: THE SUBJECT

Derrida closes his text with a reflection on the question of the signature in terms of the thesis that Austin maintains in the fifth lecture of *HTW*.

The conception of the signature outlined by Austin illuminates the irreducible anchoring of his whole theory of speech acts in the metaphysics of presence, in this case, the presence of the subject of utterance during his entire performative act. The insistence of presence, functioning as a general paradigm of the theory, leaves the problematic of the signature largely unquestioned. Austin proposes an extremely improved explication of the signature that neglects the profound implications that resurface out of the necessity for a subject to affix his signature—or indicate his presence—on a text written by him, that is, a text that is necessarily *always already detached* from its productive source.

The signature becomes inevitable once the consciousness of the graphic rupture of presence and the threat of textual escape come to light. The signature is revealed as a double-edged phenomenon (even emblematic of differance); it appears as the affirmation of the essential link that attaches the written text to its subjective productive source (its author), and at the same time exposes the fragility of this link: if the signature must confirm the link between a written text and its author, this act can only operate against the background of an ever-latent threat of detachment and separation. This ambivalence thus exposes the peril that threatens all presence and *signs* and likewise demonstrates the failure of the pretense that an author appropriates his text completely: hence the need for a signature.

Unable to define this ambivalence, Austin, according to Derrida, remained imprisoned in the metaphysical prism of the first person. To illustrate this argument, he observes that Austin accords absolute primacy to the first-person present indicative in the active voice to describe the performative. Austin acknowledges a preference for present indicative verbs and the active voice in his analysis of the performative, which is necessarily indicated in the performative act by the fact that the utterance is an action: "Only people can effect action."

Put differently, the present indicative active is revealed as the mode of utterance most *adequate* to the performative to the extent a performative necessarily indicates the existence of an agent of the act. This preference attests to a theoretical will to attach the performative utterance to its productive source in the present of the intentional subjectivity. The privilege of subjective presence translates as the reduction of the signature to a form of sustained subjective presence.[81]

Here we find in Austin a theoretical framework identical to the one Derrida had seen at work in Condillac concerning the question of the detachment of the subject's presence in relation to signs. For "by definition, a written signature implies the actual or empirical nonpresence of the signer."[82] The problem of philosophy remains its inability to take into consideration *the event of the break* in all its specificity other than by metaphysically sealing the breach with the hypostasis of presence in its extension to writing: we find the reiteration of this gesture in Austin.[83]

To sign, however, is to mark a text with one's presence, to claim to connect it to the subjective source from which it emanates while simultaneously activating an iterable procedure[84] that destroys in advance all possibility of appropriation of the utterance by its author.

Contrary to what had been affirmed by the theoreticians of communication, like McLuhan, who sees in the television screen the declaration of the disappearance of writing, Derrida proposes for deconstruction the task of opening a new path that would allow one to apprehend the generalized infiltration of writing in all phenomena of communication. Textuality is shown as the condition of possibility and impossibility of communication via the inexhaustible iteration of the mark. In the face of such theories, Derrida's true target, hitherto largely unknown, could only react and counterattack. In claiming to expose the errors of Derrida's interpretation of Austin, Searle provided an acerbic response to Derrida of which we must now give an account.

2

Do Intentions Dissolve in Iteration?

From Différance to the Dispute (Différend)

Searle begins his response to the first part of Derrida's account by addressing two principal arguments that he believes are contained in "SEC":

(1) Writing continues to function in the radical absence of sender and receiver, and thus breaks with the logic of intended meaning and of the emission context.

(2) Writing represents the privileged mode of operation for language, which takes as its condition of possibility the iterability of its elements.

To start with, Searle takes care to challenge the argument according to which writing employs a mode of operation distinct from oral speech, since *iterability is a constitutive trait of language in general and is not a phenomenon particular to writing.*[1] Every conventional linguistic procedure is *structurally iterable*; otherwise there would be no usage rules for language. The iteration of conventional procedures *thus does not apply in particular to writing* as opposed to speech. Language itself, as a system ruled by convention, implies iteration.

Searle takes recourse to the crucial logical distinction between *type* and *occurrence* in order to bolster his argument: a type, a rule-driven usage, applies to new occurrences and repeats itself in them.[2] Derrida responds to this objection by affirming that the entire thesis of "SEC" depends on this lack of distinction between speech and writing from the perspective of iterability. Indeed, Derrida had exposed the a priori character of iterability, which is a figure for generalized citational *differance* and is applicable to language in its entirety, both written and oral. It is clear from the start that Searle's and Derrida's arguments are not situated on the same level of understanding: Searle seeks to show how Derrida generalizes specific traits of writing to all language without having demonstrated that these criteria in fact form an ensemble of predicates *specific* to writing in the first place. The problem remains (and this is what we begin to grasp as we continue to read "SEC") that Derrida generalizes a concept of writing that has nothing directly in common with the classic philosophical concept of writing that Searle employs—hence the latter's lack of understanding. Extended to the new meaning of rupture with the economy of *presence*, writing is the Derridean concept par excellence; it has nothing in common with Condillac's concept of writing as communication, which Derrida had taken care to distance himself from.

In Searle's analysis, the second Derridean criterion for identifying a difference between the regimes of writing and speech is *absence*: "Is it absence, the absence of the receiver from the sender? Again, clearly not. Writing makes it possible to communicate with an absent receiver, but it is not necessary for the receiver to be absent. Written communication can exist in the presence of a receiver, as for example, when I compose a shopping list for myself or pass notes to my companion during a concert or lecture."[3] Searle's argument is this: absence is not a *systematic* component of writing. Using our own analysis of "SEC," we can anticipate Derrida's response here: Searle is still speaking of an absence that *can be compensated* and does not take into consideration the meaning of the *break* with presence that the written sign's possible *detachment* represents. Indeed, "*Sec never said* that this absence is *necessary*, only that it is *possible* (Sarl agrees) and that this possibility must therefore be taken into account: it pertains, *qua possibility*, to the structure of the mark as such, i.e., to the structure precisely of its iterability. And hence it must not be excluded from the analysis of this structure."[4] Thus writing "*must be able*: to function in the absence of. . . . But this does not mean that it does, *in fact*, necessarily function in the absence of. . . ."[5]

This possibility, however, affects every mark *from the inside* such that a mark emitted *even in the presence of the speaker remains subject to this possibility of being detached from him*. The *possibility* of absence cannot be removed—except in an abstract definition of writing that restricts absence to a contingent accident—if only because the *possibility* of absence in writing maintains its position within it as a persistent *menace* whose persistence is revealed as *constitutive* of the scriptural experience in general.

One cannot write without seeing this possibility of the demobilization of the sign as a kind of test (hence those phenomena such as the compulsion to seal, to sign, to affix the seal of one's presence that Derrida describes). Impossible to eliminate, this possibility affects every presence and provokes unconsciously and in advance its own dissolution because the trace is characterized *precisely* by its indifference, in its capacity for citational iteration, to the speaker's presence.

Because the menace of separation is *constant* in writing, writing is revealed *above all* to produce disconnection and etiolation in presence: presence cannot be totally homogenous, that is, completely protected from the risk of its own dissipation, if the *possibility* of writing as iteration remains irreducibly tied to it. Speech acts are equally subject to this possibility because parasitic and nonserious cases still remain *inevitably possible* in the economy of a theory of the *speech act*,[6] and thus mark in advance the impossibility of stabilizing the logic of intention and meaning. Thus the same goes for the "shopping list for myself" that Searle evokes, for Derrida continues: "*At the very moment* 'I' make a shopping list, I know (I use 'knowing' here as a convenient term to designate the relations that I necessarily entertain with the object being constructed) that it will only be a list if it implies my absence, if it already detaches itself from me in order to function beyond my 'present' act and if it is utilizable at another time, in the absence of my-being-present-now."[7]

The central thesis of Derrida's entire enterprise is situated right here: presence is never a *continuous* phenomenon. To think that intentional presence could maintain itself *as such*, identical to itself, in signs destined to *spread out* across time and space is thus to reason by hypostasis. As a consequence, this dissemination of written traces annihilates the metaphysical fantasy of the voice's universal extension and the ontology of truth that is its corollary.

The reactivation of presence implies from the start an irremediable loss, a known default of presence that justifies the birth of the written sign destined to play the role of substitute, of guard for a presence that is in danger and hence for this very reason always *already lost*.

The written sign always intervenes against the background of this menace at the moment when philosophy becomes conscious of the precarious position of presence and the impossibility of maintaining it. One commonly caricatures Derrida's position by claiming he argues that presence does not exist. On the contrary, Derrida is a *thinker of presence*; he is even *the* thinker of presence, that is, the only thinker to have sided with the temporary fragility of presence.

To write a *shopping list* is to recognize, despite oneself, the impossibility of maintaining self-presence: the "I" that writes the list and the "I" that receives it are of course two moments of the same "I," yet the presence of the one writing is not reducible to the presence of the other "reactivating" a defunct presence. The space that intervenes between these two moments marks the fundamental heterogeneity of presents that are destined to succeed one another in a discontinuous fashion and thus to ruin the continuous presence of the present.[8]

ITERABILITY AND PERMANENCE

Another important point of Searle's critique: Derrida confuses *iterability* with *permanence*. Indeed, according to Searle, even if iterability is not a predicate of graphemes, it is still true that writing *assures a permanence of discourse in time*.

For Searle, permanence, not iterability, is the grounds for explaining the detachment of utterance from its productive origin. Absence is indeed the *constitutive* trait of writing's permanence, for writing contains a sum of acts detached from the initial contexts of production and *independent* of these. The author of writing is *systematically absent* regardless of whether he is alive or dead. For even alive, the author will not be able to *reassume authorship* of the sum of linguistic acts that his text contains (especially if it is an extended text such as a book). The written text represents a mode of existence of acts that are not dependent on the hyperbolic perpetuation of the author's presence. Only the reading of a text gives access to the ensemble of speech acts that the author has placed there. This means that the written text in fact functions in the absence of its author, whose *presence* does not suffice to assure the recapitulation of the totality of acts that forge the text. Here Searle distinguishes clearly between *presence* and *permanence*. The text's permanence owes nothing to the author's presence; it guarantees the maintenance of speech acts beyond presence. Splashing about in a deep pool of confusion, however, Derrida, still according to Searle, attributes to iteration what in reality belongs to the *permanence* of the written text, that is, its power to detach itself from presence. For Searle, the text is a reservoir of past speech acts *preserved* beyond the living presence of the author, who has no need to respond to the illocutionary value of the signs he once deployed because otherwise the act of writing a text would no longer make any sense. It is therefore not iteration, or the reproducibility of the text in multiple copies, that assures its detachment from locutionary presence, but rather the *permanence* of past speech acts contained and preserved by the text and the text alone, independently of the author's presence. What is Derrida's response? Derrida thinks that Searle imputes to him a theory of permanence that has never been mentioned in "SEC" or in any other of his works. Derrida does not believe in permanence; what he calls "remaindrance" [*restance*] does not describe in any way the permanence of the text. "Remaindrance" is in no way permanent because it rests on the exhaustion of presence in the mark. It is in fact true that Searle does not understand this concept of "remaindrance" because he interprets it in terms of a permanence that Derrida has never invoked. We can see here the clash of two visions of the text. On the one side, Searle's vision attributes to the text the capacity to store intentional meanings produced by an author, whose disappearance does nothing to take away from the pragmatic value of the acts. The text's capacity to preserve meaning allows it to be understood by successive generations of future readers *as the same text* [*à l'identique*]. On the other side, Derrida's vision poses the *impossibility of the preservation of speech acts in all their integrity* once these are detached from the living presence of the author. For Derrida, Searle is merely rehabilitating the hypostasis of continuous presence, which reduces the text to an avatar of speech. Derrida thus denies, against Searle's imputation, that he confuses iterability and permanence; iterability in fact shatters every form of permanence from the inside. In reality, for Derrida, these two notions are opposed, whereas for Searle they are articulations of each other.

Let us return to Searle's argument that there is a difference, missed by Derrida, between permanence and iterability; this leads Searle to criticize Derrida's argument according to which it is possible to generalize the traits of the text to all speech acts. For if a text is "weaned from its origin"[9] because of its permanence, by contrast an oral expression is cut from its locutionary origin by citational iteration. Searle warns us, however, that "the two phenomena operate on quite different principles:"[10] citation has nothing "graphematic" about it—Searle takes up Derrida's term in order to use it against him. Citation has nothing to do with writing. On the contrary, it is one of the possible consequences of a use of language that is merely separated from its representational function.[11] For Searle, language cannot be reduced to signification; language has a materiality that is part of its own functional system, which does not therefore require any analogy with writing. The *means* of representation (the occurrences of signs) can be subject to proper usage that is independent of the signification to which Derrida, with the accusation of "logocentrism," systematically reduces every theory of language. Citation is not an effect of writing, but rather a logical consequence of language as a system of representation. In every linguistic system, one can demonstrate an occurrence independently of its type.[12] Derrida therefore confuses, first, permanence with iterability, two incomparable phenomena, in order to think absence. Second, he confuses the grapheme with the occurrence, even as the type/occurrence distinction belongs to the *interior* of language as a system of representation.

What is Derrida's response on this count? According to Derrida, Searle obliterates the nonclassical meaning around which "SEC" configures its theme of writing as "remaindering" that comes to destabilize every philosophical system that rests on well-established distinctions. Searle understands the concept of writing in the sense of what Derrida calls phonetic writing, as the instrumental doublet

of the voice. Thus the notion of the "graphematic" as Searle understands it has no relation to the concept that Derrida mobilizes.
Derrida argues that Searle has misconstrued things by relying on a
conception of writing that "SEC" has deconstructed.

Nevertheless, the critique remains interesting. Derrida understands as graphematic everything intrusive in language with its
nonpresence and difference. But such an intrusion depends on a
certain number of presuppositions to which Searle subscribes: first
of all, the fact that language, outside of deconstruction, is defined
systematically as an apophantic teleology. Searle's argument proves
here precisely the contrary; the linguistic system includes the possibility that it not "use" but merely "mention" its elements *independently of the problematic of their signification*. Only deconstruction
considers signification the universal paradigm of every linguistic
system. In reality, *to mention* is also one of the ruled usages of language and is not by any means constitutive of a *subversive* or *deconstructive* element.

This is why Searle's argument that Derrida confuses iterability and
writing can also function as an argument against the Derridean definition of writing; iteration has nothing to do with a scission within the
linguistic system provoked by an "arch-writing." Derrida believes that
every language [*langue*] and every system of language [*langage*] is ruled by
the exclusive primacy of signification, but this is not true: the linguistic
system also regulates the repetition of its elements through *mention*.

We will now see, however, why Derrida thinks that Searle's argument nonetheless remains attached to the presupposition of presence and, more specifically, of the intentional presence from which
the Derridean project seeks to liberate language.

INTENTIONALITY AND ITERATION

As we have seen, Searle does not subscribe to the Derridean concept of writing; Derrida interprets this refusal as Searle's misunderstanding of the true issues in "SEC." It seems to me that if Searle does not give any credit to Derrida's concept of writing, he also has deeper theoretical reasons—Searle refuses categorically the deactivation of intentionality in writing:

> Does the fact that writing can continue to function in the absence of the writer, the intended receiver, or the context of production show that writing is not a vehicle of intentionality? It seems to me quite plain that the argument that the author and intended receiver may be dead and the context unknown or forgotten does not in the least show that intentionality is absent from written communication.[13]

The argument here is clear: intentionality in written communication *does not depend on the living presence of its author* because *written propositions contain* his discursive intentions such that it is always possible to understand a text even after its author is dead. From a Derridean perspective, one would find here, in addition to the classic intentionalist argument that, as we have seen, Derrida critiques in "SEC," the Searlean argument of permanence previously mentioned, according to which a text constitutes a reservoir of past intentional acts conserved beyond the effective presence of its author:

> ask yourself what happens when you read the text of a dead author. Suppose you read the sentence, "On the twentieth of September

1793 I set out on a journey from London to Oxford." Now how do you understand this sentence? To the extent that the author said what he meant and you understand what he said you will know that the author intended to make a statement to the effect that on the twentieth of September 1793, he set out on a journey from London to Oxford, and the fact that the author is dead and all his intentions died with him is irrelevant to this feature of your understanding of his surviving written utterances.[14]

Searle remains attached to a model based on the *understanding* of intentions deposited in a text: decipherable at any time and *independently* of the effective presence that originally produced it. Nevertheless, the argument Searle invokes to defend the *communicational vocation* of writing is based on the crucial philosophical thesis that Searle exposes in *Speech Acts*: "The principle of expressibility" according to which "whatever can be meant can be said."[15] This principle, however, also functions in reverse: if whatever can be meant can be said, then inversely, everything that is said—following conventional semantic rules—is *systematically* reattachable to one or more intentions. Understanding a text, therefore, amounts to understanding a convention, that is, for Searle, *an intention*. Certainly, this intention will be well or less well expressed, but infelicity of expression remains radically *contingent*. For a sentence that does not clearly express my intention *can systematically* be replaced with a sentence that expresses *explicitly* my illocutionary intention: "even though I do not say exactly what I mean, it is always possible for me to do so—if there is any possibility that the hearer might not understand me, I may do so."[16] This means that for Searle the absence that Derrida tells us about is never an essential determination, nor is it the intimate unspeakable law of all language that rules through citational reproduction; absence reveals itself rather to be systematically surmountable thanks to the "principle of expressibility":

> But even in cases where it is in fact impossible to say exactly what I mean it is in principle possible to come to be able to say exactly what I mean. I can in principle if not in fact increase my knowledge of the language, or more radically, if the existing language or existing languages are not adequate to the task, if they simply lack the resources for saying what I mean, I can in principle at least enrich the language by introducing new terms or other devices into it.[17]

Here we thus see appear the central nerve of the opposition between Derrida and Searle: if Searle admits to the difficulty of grasping clearly and distinctly the intention of an interlocutor, this intentional absence in utterances remains purely *contingent. It does not threaten in any way the process of intentionality*, which will always be able to reassert itself through the systematic possibility of an adequate reformulation since, as Searle affirms, "there are a series of analytic connections between the notion of speech acts, what the speaker means, [and] what the sentence (or other linguistic element) uttered means."[18]

For Searle, the break advocated by Derrida never hinders the meaning and the possibility of going back *rightly* to the intentions that were at its origin.[19] And even when it is not achieved de facto, this possibility of understanding the intentions contained in a sentence remains for Searle a *transcendental possibility*. Our inability to grasp the intention in the meaning of an utterance may be due to the *nonexplicit* character of the utterance, but *never* to the utterance's intentional indetermination.

In the reply, Searle can hence continue his argumentation in this way:

> But suppose you decide to make a radical break—as one always can—with the strategy of understanding the sentence as an utterance of a man who once lived and had intentions like yourself and just think of it as a sentence of English, weaned from all production or origin, putative or otherwise. Even then there is no getting away from intentionality, because *a meaningful sentence is just a standing possibility of the corresponding (intentional) speech act.* To understand it, it is necessary to know that anyone who said it and meant it would be performing that speech act determined by the rules of the languages that give the sentence its meaning in the first place.[20]

The comprehension of an enunciation is based on an inference that is *rightly* capable of taking us from the meaning back to the intention of the sender.

What will Derrida's counteroffensive be? I have anticipated many of his arguments in my account of "SEC," but let us look at how Derrida turns them specifically against Searle. First of all, Derrida wants to establish a parallel between the Searlean argument concerning written communication and Husserl's thesis in *The Origin of Geometry*. Derrida adds, however, that his work criticizing intentionality was not an attempt to emancipate completely his own theory from the intentionalist paradigm, but rather an attempt to call into question in intention or intentionality "their *telos*, which orients and organizes the movement and the possibility of a fulfillment, realization, and *actualization* in a plenitude that would be *present* to and identical with itself."[21] This statement tends to confirm my own hypothesis that consists in seeing in the deconstructive gesture a new conception of intentionality modeled on the index and an abandonment of the expressionist model,[22] to which Searle (according to Derrida) continues to recur. This is why I insist on this point in spite of the risk of repeating myself: Searle as well as Derrida *both remain thinkers attached to the concept of intentionality*. Derrida makes explicit here deconstruction's key argument for a teleologically insurmountable tension between intentional presence and the signifiers of language, recognized as graphemes: in other words, carriers of a force of detachment with respect to all presence.[23] Once this regime of graphematic functioning has been recalled, Derrida attempts to respond by taking into account Searle's remark; at bottom, it is true that "it can happen that a mark functions without the sender's intention being actualized, fulfilled, and present, and which *to this extent* must be *presumed*."[24] As surmountable as Searle would like to believe this absence to be, a belief that presumes an intention behind the utterance, its condition of possibility is precisely that an intention can be detached from the signs that it orders. Searle, however, recognizes this possibility of absence but compensates for it with a normative theory in which the nonidentification of meaning happens to be, *by right*, always surmountable through the possibility of its explicit reformulation. For Derrida, the mere possibility of the failure to express an intention in the enunciation, a possibility that Searle is obliged to acknowledge, suffices to postulate the irreducible persistence of a certain absence. Derrida, though, objects that "one could still say: it does not *in fact always* happen like that"; in other words, it is not true that expression *always fails*. As we have seen, for Derrida, *possibility* makes the *law*, because it reveals the insurmountable divergence of legality between the level of presence and that of signifiers: Derrida tells us that "we must pass to possibility qua necessity, and moreover, we must recognize an irreducible contamination or parasitism between the two possibilities and say: 'to one degree or another that always happens, necessarily, like that': by virtue of the iterability which, in every case, forms the structure of the mark, which always divides or removes intention, preventing it from being fully present to itself in the actuality of its aim, or of some intended meaning."[25] Nevertheless, a set of theoretical misunderstandings interferes with this discussion and causes, on Derrida's side, some questionable interpretations. First questionable interpretation: Searle's reworking of Austin's theory of speech acts in light of intentionality confirms, for Derrida, his own intentionalist reading of Austin. Second problematic interpretation, which should not be underestimated: by "Husserlizing" all forms of intentionality, Derrida, who knew neither *Speech Acts* nor *Expression and Meaning* before working on his own response to Searle, has been led to caricature Searle's true position. The debate with Searle quickly transforms into a reiteration of the debate with phenomenology, which shows yet again the strong anchor attaching deconstruction to the work of Husserl, here through the instrumentalization of Austin's and Searle's theses.[26]

On this point, however, Derrida cannot help but propose a questionable interpretation with regard to Searle's theory. For the latter, by the way, the whole purpose of the critique of Grice is to show that intention does not simply add itself on top of the semantic conventions of language. In Searle, intentionality is not an act that comes to constitute signification from the outside; it is not detachable as "presence" from linguistic conventions. The phenomenological model to which Derrida refers, however, is clearly the one that he had exposed in *Voice and the Phenomenon*, that is, a scheme based on the spiritual action of a will that invests the signs of language with its "presence." This voluntarist scheme is not at all applicable to Searle, for whom intentions are not to be found *behind* the utterance but to be understood as its very content.

In *Speech Acts*, Searle praises Grice for having placed the communication of intentions between speakers at the heart of his theory of language. There thus exists for these two authors a fundamental relationship between signification and intentionality: to understand signification is to understand an intended meaning transmitted to an interlocutor with the help of indexical clues that complement the conventional meaning of the enunciation. The question, which will also come to break up the Searle/Grice relationship, remains the following: are intentions transmitted *perlocutionarily*, in other words, *by* an effect produced by the speaker on the listener that is exterior to the functioning of linguistic conventions (Grice's position), or on the contrary are intentions expressed *by* the conventions themselves (Searle's position)?

For Searle, to speak, to mobilize the conventions of language, *is already to demonstrate an intention to signify something*: signification is not an *effect*; it does not emanate from a perlocutionary force that *indicates a locutionary presence exterior to the enunciation*. Signification is a matter of conventional force, in other words, a force that is illocutionary from the start and does not have as an operator (as is the case for Grice and what Derrida thinks is the case for the theories of Austin and Searle) the *presence* that a speaker exhibits of his discursive intention outside the conventions mobilized in the proposition. For Searle it suffices to understand the sentence in order to understand its pragmatic value (or force). In this way, Searle's theory reduces considerably the importance of the context of enunciation, that is, of indexical *presence*. Indeed, the reference to context is not required in order to understand sentences unless the illocutionary act remains implicit or equivocal. But as we have seen previously, nothing prevents the amelioration of illocutionary expressivity as long as it is permitted by usage that conforms to conventions. In an implicit utterance I can take recourse to the context if the phrases are indexical. But indexicality and indirection (implying a speculation about communicational intentions) are phenomena that can be *rightly eliminated* in the conventional explication of intentions.

Such is the radicalness of Searle's thesis: enunciatory presence is not the privileged element from which one can understand intentions; the true topos of the intelligibility of intentions is convention. The conventional rules of language suffice to express our discursive intentions. Intention does not come from the outside to apply itself; it is not behind usage but rather *at the same level* as conventions themselves. Thus Searlean intentionality has nothing of the voluntarism that Derrida generalizes and brings as an accusation against the theoreticians of speech acts. It is in this sense that one must understand Searle's reproach of Derrida. Searle is not at all being naive on this point; on the contrary, he is in my opinion very lucid as far as the limits of Derrida's interpretation of intentionality are concerned: Derrida rejects the idea that an intention could be expressed in a sentence endowed with meaning, even if this sentence is *cut off* from its initial context of enunciation, simply because Derrida refuses to admit that intention, for Searle, does not depend *on presence* but only *on conventions.* The author does not need to "be there" to produce indexical clues of intentional presence, as is the case in the work of Grice: the usage of rules and conventions suffices for Searle. To understand a convention is to reach illocutionary intention; there is no need to make this intentionality dependent on a living presence that would animate or spiritually vivify the signs mobilized in enunciation. In this way, if intentional presence remains a precarious event, as Derrida has adequately demonstrated, the conventions of a language, which can certainly be reformed, remain nonetheless *stable,* remain more or less the same from one historical moment (the moment of the context of production for the written sentence, "On the twentieth of September 1793 I set out on a journey from London to Oxford") to another (the moment of reception, that is, today). For Searle, there is no effect of intention external to the enunciation that expresses it. The sign is never the relay of an animating presence by which it obtains its value as a sign. It suffices for the sign to be used according to a certain procedure for it to be endowed with an intentional meaning, which itself is never a matter of the extended, living presence of its sender. Through its stability, convention guarantees the transmission of intentional content in a process that is perfectly independent of the life of its sender.

Derrida's thesis concerning intentionality amounts to making presence the *norm of meaning,* whereas Searle thinks that it is *convention* which assigns intentional impact to an enunciation. On this point, for Searle: intention is not an instance situated behind the sentence like a presence that the sentence reflects through its meaning; intentionality of meaning is subjugated not to the presence of the sender (which, once dissipated, gives back to signs their semantic errancy), but rather only to conventional procedures whose permanence, with respect to their corresponding intentional values, remains perfectly indifferent to the hyperbolic survival of the sender:

> A *meaningful sentence is just a standing possibility of the corresponding (intentional) speech act.* . . . There are two obstacles to understanding this rather obvious point, one implicit in Derrida, the other explicit. The first is the illusion that somehow illocutionary intentions if they really existed or mattered would have to be something that *lay behind* the utterances, some inner pictures animating the visible signs. But of course in serious literal speech the sentences are precisely the realizations of the intentions: there need be no *gulf* at all between the illocutionary intention and its expression. The sentences are, so to speak, *fungible intentions* [my emphasis]. Often, especially in writing, one forms one's intentions (or meanings) in the process of forming the sentences: there need not be two separate processes.[27]

Searle's theory radically challenges the Derridean thesis of "presence" in order to think intentionality; these are two dimensions without any systematic connection, for as Searle continues: "But in fact rather few of one's intentions are ever brought to consciousness as intentions. Speaking and writing are indeed conscious intentional activities, but the intentional aspect of illocutionary acts does not

imply that there is a separate set of conscious states apart from simply writing and speaking."[28]

Derrida's defense relies on a critique that in my opinion marks
his embarrassment when faced with Searle's argument. This critique
rests on the problem of the underestimation of indexicality with
respect to the absolute primacy accorded to intention. In Searle's
theory, one need only refer to the context in order to understand
sentences when the intention is not explicit in the enunciation,
but these cases can be eliminated by expressibility. One of Searle's
strong theses in *Speech Acts* rests on placing context and indexicality in the background. Indeed, recourse to context is not necessary
to determine the illocutionary force of the sentence *except in cases in
which the performative is not explicit*. By making the performative explicit,
one should be able to eliminate any recourse to context and to
indexicality. This is the Searlean thesis, however, that embarrasses
Derrida; it has catastrophic consequences for the preservation of his
own intentionalist reading of speech acts. Indeed, Derrida affirmed
in "SEC" that the mark could be detached from its context of enunciation, that is, from the intentional presence of the produced act.
Here Searle, by detaching intention from the context and by reattaching it to conventions, separates that which in Derrida remained
assimilated, in other words, *intention* and *presence* (the living moment
that produces enunciation). The present context of the production
of enunciation remains very secondary with respect to the intentions of discourse that, if they are made explicit, no longer need to
refer back to context.

This is why Derrida plays here the indignant orthodox Austinian; to defend Austin against Searle becomes his last recourse in

maintaining his own interpretation. Lest his own reading of the performative break down, it is necessary that intentionality be always attached to the context of enunciation, in other words, to presence. Intention is connected, for Derrida, to the circumstance of enunciation (to presence), whereas for Searle, it is to the *content* of the proposition, which is by no means dependent on presence.

Searle sees the existence of a contextual but not intentional difference between speech and writing, which means that intention is no longer dependent on presence. Hence it is possible to maintain the intentional integrity of written communication: "What differs in the two cases is not the intentions of the speaker but the role of the context of the utterance in the success of the communication."[29] Derrida rejects this thesis and affirms that he has never maintained it because he obviously does not believe it: his theory of the mark should replace the intentionalist paradigm.

Searle, however, does not accuse Derrida of subscribing to this thesis, but rather of reducing every intentionalist thesis to a caricature, to this psychologism of intentions. Searle indeed makes a claim for a *conventionalism of intentions*, for the *radical entanglement of intentions in the conventional rules of discourse* such that Searle *too* abandons the psychological model. The *preservation of intentions* in discourse no longer depends on the condition that intentions precede semantic conventions.

Now Derrida reacts here in two ways, each of which is contestable: on the one hand, he accuses Searle of accusing him of psychologizing even though his theory of the trace vaunts itself as overcoming intentionality—he therefore does not understand the meaning of Searle's critique and sticks to his definition of intentionality—and, on the other hand, he commits the error that he accuses Searle of committing, that is, he accuses him of being a psychologist because he is an intentionalist.[30]

ON THE USE/MENTION DISTINCTION

All these differences engender another crucial point of divergence that precedes the discussion of Derrida's reading of Austin. Searle does not understand at all Derrida's argument that an utterance cut off from its original context of production engenders an undetermined and inexhaustible multiplicity of significations: Let us recall that Derrida gave, without being able to identify the original context of production, three equivalent significations to the phenomenologically ungrammatical utterance "the green is or." Among them, "the green is or" could signify an "example of ungrammaticality." According to Searle, however, Derrida's argument here does not hold because the utterance "the green is or" has no signification at all: it thus does not signify an "example of ungrammaticality." "The green is or" has no signification to the extent that it does not amount to a *utilization* of language but rather to a *mention*. Derrida's problem resides in his ignorance of this crucial distinction: citation is a mention; it is thus deprived of signification. Derrida, though, inscribes citation in the space of multivalence, thus *in the terrain of signification*. Mention and citation have, for Searle, nothing to do with signification: they represent a particular use of language that must be recognized as such. This is, moreover, the entire meaning of his violent criticism of Russell and Tarksi in *Speech Acts*.[31]

In this same paragraph Searle lets us understand, against the theory of proper nouns, that there are nonreferential illocutionary usages in which the sentence is deactivated semantically. This can explain Searle's reason for not accepting the thesis of a generalized citationality: citation is a particular case of the mention of language that enjoys its own legitimacy on a level that is radically *nonsemantic*. In the absence of a serious consideration of the watertight linguistic barrier that separates the semantic use of words from their mention, Derrida is led to transform every case of mention into a use. Indeed, for Derrida, a cited or grafted utterance remains open to a semantic multivalence, an undefined openness of citation to a horizon of meaning that the *use/mention* distinction should prohibit. Hence Searle's violent reaction to Derrida's laxity: citation *mentions* a sentence and *never uses it*, that is, one cannot make citation signify anything whatsoever. Because of his theory of contextual dissemination and the semantic multivalence of cited utterances, Derrida stands accused by Searle of violating the distinction between *use* and *mention*.

For Derrida, a graft is always possible onto a context in which the sentence will begin to signify, and this mere possibility forbids one from pronouncing judgment on the meaning of the sentence, not to speak of rehabilitating the criteria of presence, as Searle does in Derrida's account. Searle does this in the first place by constructing his distinction between use and mention against the theory that makes mention a (proper) name, in order to counter the argument of an infinite regression of citation to which this theory can lead.[32] Searle goes to war against the abusive proliferation of quotation marks, which the theory of the proper name inevitably generates through its incapacity to take the true logical status of the occurrence into consideration, which is never that of a specific type.

Derrida's approach, even if it has little to do with this theory of the proper name stigmatized by Searle in *Speech Acts*, becomes in the reply the target of this critique since it considers the *occurrence* (what Derrida will call in his neophenomenological vocabulary an "index") as a *type*, that is, as a *larger semantic structure*. Derrida lets us see the terms with which Searle judges the infinite multiplication of quotation marks: "He finds this point of view 'absurd' and he adds (but why?) that 'it is not harmlessly so,' having 'infected other areas of the philosophy of language.'"[33] But what is the criterion for this judgment? It is "normal use": "The fact is, we already have conventions governing the use of quotation marks. One (only one) of them is that words surrounded by quotation marks are to be taken as talked about (or quoted, etc.) and not *as used by the speaker in their normal use*."[34] On the pretext of giving citation the status of a concept (mention), Searle reiterates the most classic metaphysical gesture of the repression of citational proliferation by defending the watertight seal that distinctly separates normal use on the one side from parasitical citation on the other. However, what criterion distinguishes between the normal and the abnormal? Here is where we find the recourse to a metaphysical distinction.[35] What is obvious here is the recourse to a usage that is more normal than another, a usage normalized by the primacy accorded to the presence that masters meaning in the univocality of its determination. Citational multivalence appears henceforth as a menacing phenomenon whose status will always be relativized with respect to the most "ordinary" usages, the best-mastered usages of language. But conventions cannot be completely adequate, according to Derrida, "if language can always" normally "become" abnormally "its own object" through the structural iterability of the mark.

Here we are then at the question of "serious discourse" and the critique that Derrida proposes of Searle's recourse to this notion.

SERIOUS DISCOURSE AND ITERATION

What is a serious discourse once it is fatally condemned to iteration? The theory of serious discourse is not possible unless it rests on idealization. In Searle, as in Austin previously, one sees at work the same gesture excluding the nonserious on the basis of purely ideal dichotomies in which strict and literal usages can be distinguished, in a theoretically decisive manner, from usages that are nonserious, metaphorical, ironic, and so on. The same serious utterance, however, can always be repeated as a joke in an ironic context or in parody. One and the same utterance can be uttered seriously or nonseriously: no criterion attaches a sequence of signs employed in an utterance to a *definitive* illocutionary value. Against this obvious fact, one finds in Searle—according to Derrida—a logic of intention that permits one to implement value distinctions on utterances that, in themselves, are intrinsically undecidable before this psychological intervention. The idealization thus consists in the privilege given to one usage over others; it aims to cast the original semantic dissemination into an axiological hierarchy that judges one usage more "proper" than others. According to Derrida, one finds here a psychological logic disavowed by Searle: utterances do not derive their seriousness from criteria internal to language but from an external intended meaning [*vouloir-dire*] that imposes a privileged meaning [*sens*] which the utterances themselves do not have.[36] From a *graphic* perspective of the utterance, no usage can have privilege over another. It is from the perspective of *intention* that distinctions between serious and nonserious usages can be discerned. The more an utterance is vested with the presence of its speaker, the more serious it is compared to a nonserious usage, like a stage play in which the actor does not implicate himself intentionally in the utterances that he recites (he does not say them "for real"). The actor has no intention of really demanding what he demands on the stage (let us suppose that his role dictates that he make a demand at a certain moment); he is only reciting a memorized text. The idealization consists in giving priority to one usage over another. This priority will always be attributed to the self-aware and self-present configuration of language such that every definition of language has to be based on this modal configuration of presence elevated to a paradigm.

Everything that this idealization has left aside should be recognized as an ensemble of contingent distortions of normal usage that only externally affect the speech act, maintained by theory in its most intact purity as a vehicle of intentions. This strategy has permitted the elimination of a danger that would have consisted in accepting the reversibility of the present speech act with its ever-possible degradation, its ever-menacing distortion through its difference from itself.

How does one render null and void the system of oppositions between serious and nonserious, literal and metaphoric?

The functioning of the mark. By its iterability, every mark used in a speech act is always already a re-mark. As a re-mark, the mark dissolves the momentous plentitude of the present act: "Once it is iterable, to be sure, a mark marked with a supposedly 'positive' value ('serious,' 'literal,' etc.) can be mimed, cited, transformed into an 'exercise' or into 'literature,' even into a 'lie'—that is, it can be made to carry its other, its 'negative' double. But iterability is also, by the same token, the condition of the values said to be 'positive.' The simple fact is that this condition of possibility is structurally divided or 'differing-deferring' [*différante*]."[37]

The expression "condition of possibility" is clearly affirmed here by Derrida. The values of the accident, the nonserious, the metaphoric, and repetition win against those of truth in a broad sense, in the sense that the former condition the latter at the source. The Derridean perspective is indeed genetic in this sense: it is a matter of returning to the conditions of possibility of truth. It is worth summoning once again the metaphor of the actor: one understands how the actor accomplishes his first performance on stage, which constitutes an event ("opening night") by repeating the rehearsals that preceded it. The opening of the "opening night" is repetition (rehearsal).[38] *It is not repetition that repeats the event, but the event that repeats repetition.* In the speech act, we perform the event by repeating a procedural text that is intrinsically iterable.

THE STAKES AT PLAY IN THE UNCONSCIOUS

The reference to Freud constitutes one of the fundamental dimensions of the deconstructive dynamic, principally through the renewal of the concept of time (the transition from presence to diffe*r*ance) that Derrida suggests in his argument against phenomenology.[39]

Thus the Freudian theory of the unconscious appears very early for Derrida as a framework that paves the way for the rupture with the logic of presence, which had formerly been content to define the unconscious in a totally reductive fashion as a form of nonconsciousness.

For Derrida, the unconscious must be understood as an effect of the general movement of differance as "trace," a notion that Derrida takes from Freud in order to use it against him, at least in part (Derrida refuses the risk of the substantiation of the unconscious that he perceives in Freud).[40]

Nevertheless, the affinities outweigh the disagreements, which allows deconstruction to inherit principles acquired by psychoanalysis and to maintain thereby a lively criticism of the naive assumptions of the philosophy of consciousness. A common theoretical front thus unites deconstruction and psychoanalysis. This subtle and efficient alliance redeploys here its argumentative arsenal in order to rout Searle's intentionalist approach to speech acts. Let us recall that Searle had retorted to Derrida that he wrongly supports the illusion according to which "intentions must all be conscious. But in fact rather few of one's intentions are ever brought to consciousness as intentions."[41] I have already offered an interpretative solution to this remark consistent with the theses developed in *Speech Acts* by showing that Searle defends a conventionalist, not a representationalist, theory of intentionality. Derrida here understands the accusation as if it were addressed to the thesis that he defends in "SEC," whereas Searle is only pointing out what in his eyes demonstrates the reduction of the intentionalist thesis to presence.

Derrida reacts brutally because he believes that Searle is accusing him of not knowing about the unconscious.[42]

Once again it is Austin whom Derrida convokes against Searle; Austin's only text that traces metaphorically the theoretical contours of a description of the unconscious is "Three Ways of Spilling Ink."[43] Derrida returns to the argument that he had elaborated previously, according to which his own theory does not aim so much to extenuate intentionality as to accept the limits of language understood as writing: "To claim that for *Sec* all intentions are conscious is to read *à contre-pied*, fake(d) out, in the sense of Littré. For not only does *Sec* say that all intentions are *not* conscious: it says that *no* intention can *ever* be entirely conscious, fully and simultaneously present to itself. Nor is it so different from Austin, who in 'Three Ways of Spilling Ink,' asserted 'The only general rule is that the illumination (shed by intention) is always limited, and that in several ways.'"[44] Derrida has indeed discovered the passage that in Austin's doctrine is the most suggestive with regard to the existence of the unconscious in the shadow left by the limits of the glow of intention. As much as Derrida recognizes and praises Austin for having defended an idea very near to his own conception of intentionality, he disapproves of Searle's method that for him only constructs a theory destined "to keep the hypothesis of such an Unconscious at a safe distance, as though it were a giant Parasite."[45] It must be remarked here that while "SEC" took Austin as its privileged target, one notices in *Limited* that the attacks formerly destined for Austin are now reserved in an almost exclusive manner for Searle. The cause of this redirection lies, in my opinion, in Derrida's more profound understanding of Austin developed between 1971 and 1977 thanks to Derrida's discovery of the *Philosophical Papers*, unknown to him at the time of writing "SEC," which concentrates exclusively on *HTW*. Moreover, Searle's assault incited Derrida to elaborate his response and read the published works of the former. In such a way, a more subtle knowledge of Austin, accompanied by a consideration of Searle's theory, allowed Derrida to understand retroactively that the real (unconscious!) target of "SEC" was not primarily Austin but in fact Searle.

This paradoxical situation makes yesterday's enemies today's friends, and the veritable target of deconstruction now sees the light of day. In this way, if Derrida speaks of the Unconscious as a giant Parasite, it is with reference to the psychoanalytic Unconscious and not to the cognitive unconscious "that Sarl seems to envisage, as a kind of lateral, virtual potential of consciousness."[46]

For Derrida, the intentionalist theory of *Speech Acts* "condemns the unconscious as one bars access to a forbidden place."[47] It is obvious that if the values of intention and seriousness structure Searle's analytic horizon, then the psychoanalytic Unconscious can only appear as *the* parasite par excellence since it presupposes a logic of the act that subverts all intentional logic. Derrida recalls the conditions for the success of a speech act in Searle's *Speech Acts*: "the exclusion of all 'parasites,' and the necessity that speaker and hearer be 'conscious of what they are doing.'"[48] This means that speech and writing are entirely conscious procedures for Searle, whereas "SEC" had sought precisely to create for them the conditions for the articulation of "a general graphematics based not on an axiomatics confined to the 'psychology' or to the 'phenomenology' of consciousness, but on what for instance and for the instant can be called the Unconscious. This Unconscious is absolutely excluded by the axiomatics (which is also an axiology) of current speech act theory, in particular as formulated by Searle."[49]

What theoretic implications emerge from this inclusion of the Unconscious in the theory of speech acts?

Derrida's argumentation proceeds as follows: Derrida supposes that he will "seriously promise to criticize implacably each of Sarl's theses."[50] Now according to *Speech Acts* (chapter 3), such a promise cannot be seriously effectuated because it does not fulfill the conditions for the realization of a promise. It is in fact more a threat than a promise; according to Searle, there is "crucial distinction between promises on the one hand and threats on the other consisting in the fact that a promise is a pledge to do something for you, not to you."[51] The necessary conditions for the realization of a promise are not reunited: the procedure just described implies that a promise cannot be fulfilled if it is not desired by the person to whom the promise is made, and if the person who promises does not believe that his interlocutor desires that the promise be fulfilled. It is thus necessary that I be conscious of my desire to make a promise *and* of the desire of the person to whom I make this promise. If these two clauses are not respected, the promise transforms into a threat.

According to Derrida, this description of a successful promise is based on the cognitive privilege of consciousness (the consciousness to make a promise that implies the consciousness of the desire of the interlocutor). For Derrida, who deliberately makes fun of Searle/Sarl here, the whole question is: what can one know, from the point of view of the Unconscious, about Searle's desire?

At bottom, who knows that Derrida did not predict Searle's unconscious desire to be criticized? Under such circumstances, would his promise to criticize implacably each of Searle's theses become a threat? Consideration of the psychoanalytic Unconscious here blurs all the established criteria for success: for if unconscious desire is taken into consideration, the possibility of Searle's desire to be criticized by Derrida would keep his promise (to criticize implacably Searle's theses) in the state of a promise rather than change it into a threat.

But this double signification of the speech act contradicts the intentional simplicity to which Searle would like to reduce it. At the same time, this double layer of motivation (conscious and unconscious) annihilates every possibility of illocutionary identification for the fulfilled act. One thus finds here the figure of the *double bind* that belongs to the movement of differance, where contradictions imply and neutralize one another reciprocally: here the speech act reveals itself to be promise and threat *at the same time*. Starting with the parasitical intervention of the unconscious, *the meaning of the speech act is revealed as profoundly and irreducibly undecidable*. Only a gesture of theoretical elimination of the Unconscious could preserve the univocality of the act's meaning. Searle's theory thus cannot hold unless it isolates the conscious ego ideally from its psychic inscription as a whole.

Nonetheless, Derrida does not rehabilitate here a purely psychoanalytic position, for if the pure ideality of the conscious ego must be deconstructed, the same is true for the opposition between conscious and unconscious that reproduces, despite itself, the possibility of isolating the conscious sphere from the unconscious, which holds itself at a distance and only acts on consciousness from the outside. For Derrida, the alterity of consciousness must be recognized as a phenomenon *internal* to consciousness and implied by the precedence of iterability over presence. In this sense Derrida's analysis distinguishes itself from a pure psychoanalysis of the kind found in Freudian metapsychology (even if a comparison with the *Psychopathology of Everyday Life* seems to me very illuminating for an understanding of the thesis defended in "SEC").

In Derrida's account, Freud still remains too attached to a static schema of oppositions—binary (conscious/unconscious) and then ternary (id/ego/superego)—which differance reconfigures dynamically. This is why Derrida very often rejects, as he does here, the term "Unconscious" when one does not grasp this phenomenon as the effect of a more profound movement of differance, which subverts the conscious ego and its intentional services *from the inside*, without adding itself onto the ego from the outside as a distinct psychic instance.

THE MEANING OF A "FOOTNOTE" AND THE LOGICAL STATUS OF FICTION

With respect to Searle, this question takes us to his article "The Logical Status of Fictional Discourse," published in 1975 in the journal *New Literary History* and republished in *Expression and Meaning*.[52]

The fundamental thesis developed by Searle in this article is based on the identification and explication of the modal difference existing between assertive discourse and fictional discourse. The difference between these two types of discourse does not arise from an illocutionary rupture between a serious utterance and the same utterance pronounced in a fictional regime, for if this were the case, fictional discourse would be unintelligible. In fictional discourse we perform the same illocutionary acts as in assertive discourse but *follow distinct and inassimilable discursive conventions*. Searle discusses four semantic rules that determine assertive discourse.[53] A journalist, author of an assertion, must be able to answer for the truth of his discourse; this is not the case for the novelist, for example.

At the same time, it would be an error, Searle reminds us, to believe that the journalist and the novelist perform distinct illocutionary acts. The acts performed in an assertive context and those realized in a fictional context *are the same*, for "if the sentences in a work of fiction were used to perform some completely different speech acts from those determined by their literal meaning, they would have to have some other meaning."[54] Thus words used in the context of a literary work lose their ordinary meaning and, at one and the same time, their intelligibility. In such a case, it is necessary to conceive of two distinct classes of predicates to be attributed to assertive utterances and fictional utterances respectively, which is absurd since fiction *mimes* reality and can only be understood under this condition.

Searle thus advocates for the necessity of starting from the second meaning of the word "pretend" in order to grasp the discursive specificity of fictional utterances: on the one hand, to "pretend" means to deceive, but on the other to "pretend" means to play at imitating something without the intention to deceive, *in other words, without the intention to make one believe it is the truth*. The first meaning associates the act of pretending with a lie, the second liberates the act of pretending from the apophantic prism and the enunciation from the question of truth.

One must thus recommence with this second meaning: the laws that regulate the functioning of fictional discourse are based on an act of pretending inscribed in a discursive register that no longer has truth as its referent. The question of truth in such a case is deactivated and illocutionary acts are performed independently of all assertive logic. Thus "the author of a work of fiction pretends to perform a series of illocutionary acts, normally of the assertive type."[55] Here we can only witness and confirm the very clear distinction in Searle's theoretical economy between *intentionality* and *logocentric presence* since Searle thematizes here an intentional mode that no longer has anything assertive about it and *is no longer logically dependent on the question of truth*. Derrida, however, thinks that the deconstruction of truth presupposes from the start the deconstruction of the logic of "intended meaning" [*vouloir-dire*] that is rife with the metaphysics of presence. One sees here that the association of intentionality and truth is short-circuited by Searle's claim: *there are uses of intentionality that have nothing to do with assertion*. It is therefore regrettable that in his response Derrida claims to see nothing in Searle's text but a return to the most classically logocentric intentionality, even though Searle's theory of fiction goes in the exact opposite direction. One can thus certainly maintain intentionality in the case of fictional discourse, for the question of the status of fictional discourses does not lie, as Derrida believes, in the question of intentionality but in the use that one makes of this intentionality: fictional intentionality mobilizes language according to a logic different from assertive intentionality. This distinction is of crucial importance for Searle, whereas Derrida, for the sake of the internal coherence of his own philosophical logic, denies its import and pertinence.

According to Searle, textuality is a completely intentional phenomenon. Searle also situates himself at the opposite end of Derrida's thesis according to which the text implodes the homogenous and holistic movement of linguistic intentionality. Indeed, for Searle, "even so much as to identify a text as a novel, poem, or even as a text is already to make a claim about the author's intentions."[56]

The distinction between vertical and horizontal rules that Searle had already established in *Speech Acts*[57] is absolutely crucial here for an understanding of the intentional regulation of fictional discourse.

Here two regimes of conventional law are distinguished: on the one hand, the *vertical conventions* that determine the relation of utterances to the world; on the other hand, the *horizontal conventions* that "break the connections established by the vertical rules."[58]

Two important points can thus be drawn from Searle's analysis:

(1) Horizontal conventions assure a use of intentionality that no longer has anything apophantic about it.
(2) Conventions cannot be reduced to the rules of meaning.

Nevertheless, if the rules of meaning and their implied ontological engagements are deactivated, the acts themselves are not at all unreal. They are indeed realized illocutionary acts, but thanks to horizontal conventions, they have no illocutionary consequences. In this sense, it is the conventional causality discussed by Austin in *HTW*[59] that is deactivated in pretending.

The theory that Searle elaborates here is one of the most interesting in that it permits the distinction between intention and presence on the one hand and between intention and truth on the other, all terms that remain assimilated too systematically in Derrida's framework.

Does this text, however, refute Derrida's thesis or does it, on the contrary, reinforce it? There seem to be many reasons to lean toward the second hypothesis. Indeed, the existence of horizontal conventions does nothing to modify the semantic structure of the utterance. The utterance stays the same; only its usage changes such that this thesis seems to confirm Derrida's theory to the extent that one and the same utterance can be associated with different intentions (here vertical or horizontal). For this very reason the utterance can be "grafted" from one context to another since the transition from the assertive to the fictional requires only a modification of the intentional stance and not of the semantic structure of the utterance. In this sense, the utterance is truly grafted from an assertive context to a fictional context. But Searle would no doubt refuse such assimilation and invoke in this regard the dimension of constraint that horizontal conventions represent, which makes impossible the strict equivalence between serious and fictional utterances that Derrida would like to thematize. The transition from vertical conventions to horizontal conventions has nothing to do with the citational procedure that Derrida discusses.

In addition, another irreducible difference condemns in advance this kind of reconciliation: intentionality. Derrida could indeed without a doubt retort to Searle that the model invoked here remains clearly intentionalist. One sees how intentionality in Searle's sense *places itself in the service of nonserious enunciations*, a claim that Derrida challenges when he affirms that fictional utterances constitute a class of utterances that are *intentionally divested* through all the figures of repetition that fictional utterances allow (in theatrical parody, for example).

Here once again an easing of the conflict remains a chimera as Derrida seeks to show how fictional utterances exhaust intentionality in iteration, while Searle *diversifies* and *declines* intentionality *modally*, allowing him to put in play epistemic roles that are very diverse and irreducible to the sole question of truth to which deconstruction *systematically links* intentionality at the price of flattening its modal variations.

PARASITISM AND CITATION

Searle takes a stand against Derrida's lack of conceptual rigor. He holds very broadly to the fact that Derrida confuses levels of analysis that are in reality quite distinct. Among these confusions, the most notable regards the relationship between the phenomena of parasitism and citation, which Derrida wrongly assimilates. Indeed, a novelist does not *cite*; writing here has nothing to do with citationality, and an actor on stage does not cite his text either.

Fictional utterances *are not citations*. The role of horizontal conventions examined earlier is implicit here as well. In contrast to citation, which mentions language without utilizing it, the fictional utterance *does utilize language*, although the practical and ontological engagements that its acts ordinarily imply are deactivated.[60] According to Searle, Derrida confuses iterability, parasitism, and citationality. Parasitism, however, is not a "modification" of citationality, but only of iterability, that is, of the applicability of conventional rules as conditioned by their repeatability: the conventional procedure of a performative act cannot be modified from one occurrence to another. It is true that parasitism is conditioned by iterability, but this is precisely because it *utilizes* language (as opposed to citation, which mentions it).

In Searle's account, Derrida believes that parasitism reflects the iterability of language such that its exclusion by Austin implies the exclusion of the very possibility of the effectuation of the performative. Yet "this argument is not valid," for "even had Austin's exclusion of fictional discourse been a metaphysical exclusion and not a part of his investigative strategy, it would not follow from the fact that

Austin excludes parasitic discourse that he excludes any other forms of iterability."[61] It is thus necessary to distinguish between two instances of iterability: an ordinary iterability (vertical rules of linguistic usage) and a parasitic iterability (horizontal rules of linguistic usage), which are logically distinct and which must not, as in Derrida, be confused.

Searle is nevertheless ready to recognize that Derrida is not wrong in making iteration a functional principle of conventional rules, though he is quite mistaken when he assimilates iterability to citationality, for in citation one no longer utilizes linguistic conventions but mentions them. In his response to this objection, Derrida impugns Searle's accusation that he has confused parasitic discourse with citationality. On the contrary, Derrida does not make iterability the distinctive criterion between these two dimensions because for him they both belong to the general regime of iteration as *writing*: this regime determines at once the conventional rules that govern the success of the performative, and at the same time fractures this realization through the phenomena of parasitic replication that it makes possible (imitation, mime, parody).

Derrida rejects Searle's interpretation that "SEC" confuses iterability, citationality, and parasitism. When Derrida affirms that the nonserious in Austin is a matter of a "determined modification of a general citationality—or rather, of a general iterability," he adds "or rather" to prove that he does not confuse citationality and iterability.

In addition, Searle does not understand "modification" as he should, that is, as a mode of the more global movement of iteration as writing. It is in this sense that the parasitic reveals itself to be a determined mode of iteration: no parasitic usage without the general possibility of iteration. Searle is wrong to oppose modification to instantiation since parasitism and citation are in fact both modal instantiations of iteration. For Searle, parasitism proceeds from a modification of the rules of conventional usage of normal speech acts, but does not modify iteration at all because iteration conditions the conventionality of rules. Derrida radicalizes this gesture; here for him modification no longer signifies transformation, as it does for Searle, but a modality of a "transcendental," the iteration that, because it conditions every convention of ordinary linguistic usage, also deconstructs seriousness and presence. iteration applies as much to the serious (in conventions) as it does to the parasitic (in the reproduction of the serious). In both cases, it is the same effect of the *repeated* that *orders and disorders simultaneously* the normalized functioning of language.

Indeed, the Searlean thesis of the dependence of ordinary usage on iteration *necessarily implies*, for Derrida, the dependence of serious utterances on parasitism as well, that is, on iteration in general. Both the repetition of conventions in ordinary usage and the parodic or mimetic repetition in parasitic usage refer to *the same nonsimple phenomenon of generalized iteration*. It is thus not possible to distinguish them thematically as Searle does.

Searle does not therefore draw all the conclusions of the thesis that both ordinary language and parasitic language are ruled by iteration when he maintains the distinction between vertical and horizontal conventions. For Derrida, this border is undermined from the inside by iteration as writing, which gnaws away at the distinctions of iterative regimes. Horizontal convention can always be the object of a "graft" and find itself parodied in a new context that will no

longer be that of the theatrical play or novel for which the enunciation, as an effect of iteration, was initially attached since it can
never be *definitively* attached. The effects of iteration multiply indefinitely and greatly increase the phenomena of scission and overflow
as regards every conceptual distinction made (as occurs with the distinction between two modalities of convention, or iteration, vertical
and horizontal).

In this way, one can always *fictionalize fiction* because the iterative
hemorrhage has *no limit.* Generally (vertically or horizontally), conventions engender *through their iterative structure*—and without the possibility of restraining this movement—*new* repetitions that explode
the distinctions of ordinary pragmatics: thus disseminating without
restraint from the serious to the nonserious (in the case of vertical
conventions) or from the nonserious to other undetermined forms
of the nonserious (in the case of horizontal conventions).

This renewal, made possible by an attentive consideration of
the effects of iteration, causes the distinction between serious and
nonserious to explode, for there will always exist new, unpredictable
forms of the nonserious that escape the typologies described by the
theoretical discourse on the parasitic. For this reason, iteration has
an aptitude for grafting or citing in new contexts *to come* [*à venir*], still
imperceptible on the present horizon of theory represented by the
forms of enunciation reduced to the restrictive polarity of the serious
and nonserious.

There exists, therefore, a "future" of language that Derrida will
attach to the key speech act, the "promise," which should lead us to
give up, by defusing them, the logical operators that aim to atten-
uate the disseminating movement of differance, in other words,

everything that channels the effects of iteration in decisive conceptual distinctions and represses the mark's *power of novelty*.

Iteration is therefore never reducible to the iteration of the "Same," as Searle ultimately reduces it (in the identification of determined types belonging to serious or nonserious, vertical or horizontal conventions). Iteration is always an appeal to the Other, an altering breakthrough by a still-unknown event [*advenue*], still and always *to come* [*à-venir*], and thus impossible to anticipate with positivity: the repetition in iteration as produced by differance is necessarily *repetition of the Same in the Other*. What Searle fails to recognize is the connection (which he radically refuses) between iteration and citationality, for it is only under the regime of the latter that the impact of iteration can be fully understood in all its amplitude.

The critique of the analogy between writing and the parasitic constitutes the basis on which Searle builds his more global critique of Derrida. For Searle, it is not at all evident that writing represents a phenomenon parasitic on speech *in the same way* as parasitic usages are with respect to their corresponding normal usages. These cases have nothing in common for two reasons: (1) There exists a logical and necessary relation of dependence between fiction and nonfiction to the extent that the concept of fiction follows logically from the existence of the concept of normal discourse. By contrast, the concept of writing is not *necessarily* implied by the concept of oral speech. (2) Illustration of this relative independence of writing from speech can be found in cases in which it is speech that depends on writing, as in mathematical and logical symbolism. In response to this argument, Derrida refers Searle once again to "SEC," which never assimilated writing and parasitism and maintains a nuanced difference between these two associated phenomena. The fact is that for Derrida there is no unifiable concept of writing: this is the distinguishing characteristic of his method, the concept of writing itself as a pitfall that refers not only to the historical and philosophical transition from orality to the written word *but also to the impact and the effects of the necessity* of this transition, which has not been noted by philosophy for constitutive reasons. For Derrida, the advent of writing refers to a broader and ungraspable dynamic of the parasitism on presence, on the simple, on the homogenous, inflected by a large, nonsynthetic variety of manifestations: writing in the empirical sense of the word is thus only one of the modalities of a more global parasitic order.

In response, Derrida maintains that he does not see how the mathematical argument contradicts his statements; this argument only reveals Searle's ignorance of the texts of deconstruction. Indeed, on multiple occasions, Derrida had considered mathematical formalization as a model allowing the liberation of writing from phonocentrism.[62]

For Searle, iteration is a phenomenon that conditions intentionality to the extent that it is through iteration that the rules of language are applicable and the pragmatic communication of intentions becomes possible.

Derrida draws precisely the inverse conclusion; for him, iterability is not fully taken into consideration by Searle, who confuses it with repeatability,[63] with a recursive conception of rules that postulates their identity in repetition. When it is fully accepted, iterability is an opening to the advent [*venue*] of the Other: it does not repeat anything except its own alteration in the *nonidentical* of the new.

We can see how, for Searle, intentionality is connected to the rules of language, whereas for Derrida intentionality, always apprehended in light of presence, finds itself perforated and fettered by iteration, of which the repeatability of rules is only a subordinate determination, derived from the more profound power of extraction that iteration possesses as a movement of writing.

Conclusion

It is no small statement to affirm that the richness of this controversy makes ostensible not the insurmountable divergence of the continental and analytic traditions, but rather the wealth and diversity of the discussions of intentionality in the twentieth century.

More than ever, the Derrida/Searle debate seems to lay out a framework for renewed reflection on this concept. "SEC" indeed proposes a neophenomenological interpretation of Austin. Rereading his theory of the performative in light of the Husserlian concept of intentionality as presence, Derrida can critique Austin, who in his view bases the success of the performative on intentional presence: for Austin, the fact of enacting something in the world through the intermediary of language thus amounts to a cognitive mastery of the process by which the performative is accomplished, without any remainder or difference, without any distance from the conscious presence of the speaker. If it is true that in Austin the speaker must know what he is doing and what the circumstances allow him to accomplish as speech acts, it is not at all certain that the concept of "presence," whose texture remains too thick and too closely tied to phenomenology, is the best candidate for taking into account what one could identify in Austin as a "sensitivity to context" necessary for the successful functioning of ordinary linguistic activity.

Simply speaking, it is surprising to note that Searle also reinterprets Austin in light of the concept of intentionality that he, by contrast, does not take from Husserl's phenomenology—which he does not know—but rather from Paul Grice's pragmatism.

Even if Derrida and Searle agree that the performative act translates a mental intention, they do not draw the same theoretical conclusions: for Derrida, Austin's theory of the performative merely pursues a logic in which language is saturated by present and self-mastered consciousness, which his theory of writing aims to deconstruct— as it had done previously for Husserl's theory of intentionality in *Voice and Phenomenon* by taking up another aspect of Austin's theory: the primacy accorded by Austin in *HTW* to conventions and to the iteration of the processes by which the performative is accomplished, which, like the written mark, are subject to repetition.

Now the aptitude of a written mark to be repeated in its rereading or rewriting beyond intentional enunciatory presence is what allows Derrida to oppose the unity of the performative act accomplished in the present with the logic of the written text as an instance of the rupture between linguistic signs and presence.

For his part, in his response to Derrida, Searle thinks that the implied break with presence does not suppress the intentional impact of the content of a written page. If, for Derrida, a written sentence resists "full" comprehension in any reading because the subjective presence of the speaker has disappeared from the arranged signs, for Searle by contrast the pragmatic meaning of the enunciation is not threatened by writing to the extent that the reader in fact can understand precisely the semantic conventions that have been mobilized in the past by an author now detached from the acts he has accomplished.

This means that the pragmatic or intentional (what the author meant or wanted to say) value of an utterance resides for Derrida entirely in the *presence* with which the author is able to infuse a sequence of signifiers, whereas for Searle the intentional value of an utterance resides entirely in the *usage of conventions* that a proposition translates: no need in such a case to trace intentionality back to the presence of a living subjectivity preserved in written sentences. Searle thus disarticulates two notions that Derrida assimilates, namely, *intentionality* and *presence*, since for the former, the intentions of a speaker can only be grasped in terms of conventions.

This divergence is likewise reflected in the divergence that can be observed between the ways the two authors treat the problem of fiction: for Searle, fictional utterances refer to nonassertive forms of intentionality which respond to *conventions* that are distinct from those to which assertive utterances are subject. As for Derrida, he opposes fictional utterances to the very idea of intentionality, which he still understands restrictively as intentional *presence*, since such utterances seem to him to be detached from a responsibility assumed in the first person.

In fact, Derrida and Searle both turn out to be faithful to the primacy that Austin accords to conventions but in radically divergent ways, because for Searle the iteration of conventions assures the intentional intelligibility of language, whereas for Derrida, on the contrary, the iteration of conventions shows itself—going beyond Austin's work—to be in the service of a powerful subversion of the ontology of the Same: iteration always calls forth new meanings *to come* [*à venir*] beyond the predictions of a language's conventional system (which Searle, in Derrida's mind, holds to) and the performative typologies that it organizes. Without a doubt, this call to the Other, which the performative makes possible in an iteration that transcends every convention, will serve as the matrix of deconstruction's hyperbolic ethics and as the act of *promising* that will support this ethics.

Far from having been a vain quarrel, the Derrida/Searle debate has the merit of posing the question of the performative for renewed reflection on the basis of tools bequeathed by the continental tradition, addressing this question—as Derrida does—on the basis of a cross between the phenomenological problematic of intentionality and the psychoanalytic problematic of the death drive (as mortifying repetition). From our perspective, this confrontation over the performative between the pragmatism of the ordinary and continental thought, which my discussion has begun to work through, opens up to the possibility of a new inflection of the performative in its articulation at the limits of meaning, one that will nonetheless need to be reconsidered along coordinates that are no longer dependent on the reference to *the one and only* phenomenology.

Notes

FOREWORD

1. Benoît Peeters, *Trois ans avec Derrida: Les carnets d'un biographe* (Paris: Flammarion, 2010).

2. Pierre Nora, *Les Français d'Algérie, édition revue et augmentée* (Paris: Christian Bourgeois, 2012).

3. Nicholas Royle, *In Memory of Jacques Derrida* (Edinburgh: Edinburgh University Press, 2009); Peggy Kamuf, *To Follow: The Wake of Jacques Derrida* (Edinburgh: Edinburgh University Press, 2010); Geoffrey Bennington, *Not Half No End: Militantly Melancholic Essays in Memory of Jacques Derrida* (Edinburgh: Edinburgh University Press, 2010); Derek Attridge, *Reading and Responsibility: Deconstruction's Traces* (Edinburgh: Edinburgh University Press, 2010).

4. Attridge, *Reading and Responsibility*, 51.

5. Peter Sloterdijk, *Derrida, an Egyptian: On the Problem of the Jewish Pyramid* (London: Polity, 2009).

6. Alain Badiou, *Pocket Pantheon: Figures of Postwar Philosophy*, trans. David Macey (London: Verso, 2009), 125–144. This lecture was given in 2005.

7. Martin Hägglund, *Radical Atheism: Derrida and the Time of Life* (Stanford: Stanford University Press, 2008). See also his application of the logic of survival to modernist literature in Hägglund, *Dying for Time: Proust, Woolf, Nabokov* (Cambridge, Mass.: Harvard University Press, 2012).

8. See Jacques Derrida, *Learning to Live Finally*, trans. Pascale-Anne Brault and Michel Naas (Brooklyn: Melville House, 2007).

9. John Sallis, ed., *Deconstruction and Philosophy* (Chicago: University of Chicago Press, 1987).

10. Leonard Lawlor, *Derrida and Husserl: The Basic Problem of Phenomenology* (Bloomington: Indiana University Press, 2002).

11. See Raoul Moati, ed., *Autour de Slavoj Zizek: Psychanalyse, Marxisme, Idéalisme allemand* (Paris: Presses Universitaires de France, 2010); and Raoul Moati, *Evénements Nocturnes: Essai sur Totalité et Infini* (Paris: Hermann, 2012).

12. Jacques Derrida, "Afterword: Toward an Ethic of Discussion," in *Limited Inc*, trans. Samuel Weber (Evanston, Ill.: Northwestern University Press, 1998), 130.

13. Jean-Michel Rabaté, *The Ethics of the Lie* (New York: Other Press, 2007), 360–363.

14. Jacques Derrida, *The Postcard*, trans. Alan Bass (Chicago: University of Chicago Press, 1987), 136. I owe this quote to Charles Ramond's excellent *Le Vocabulaire de Jacques Derrida* (Paris: Ellipses, 2001), 53–54.

INTRODUCTION: THE CIRCUMSTANCES OF AN "IMPROBABLE" DEBATE

1. I am thinking here of Charles Ramond, who outlines certain salient aspects of the Derrida/Searle confrontation. Ramond, *Vocabulaire de Derrida* (Paris: Ellipses, 2001).

2. J. L. Austin, *How to Do Things with Words* (Oxford: Clarendon Press, 1962). Hereafter this text is abbreviated as *HTW*.

3. Austin, *Quand dire, c'est faire* (Paris: Le Seuil, 1970).

4. Jacques Derrida, *La voix et le phénomène* (Paris: Presses Universitaires de France, 1967); Derrida, *De la grammatologie* (Paris: Éditions de Minuit, 1967); and Derrida, *L'écriture et la différence* (Paris: Le Seuil, 1967). These are translated in English as

Derrida, *Voice and Phenomenon*, trans. Leonard Lawlor (Evanston, Ill.: Northwestern University Press, 2011); Derrida, *Of Grammatology*, trans. Gayatri Chakravorty Spivak (Baltimore: Johns Hopkins University Press, 1976); and Derrida, *Writing and Difference*, trans. Alan Bass (Chicago: University of Chicago Press, 1978).

5. John R. Searle, "Reiterating the Differences: A Reply to Derrida," *Glyph Review* 2 (1977): 198–208. Hereafter this text is abbreviated as "Reiterating."

6. Derrida, *Limited Inc*, trans. Samuel Weber (Evanston, Ill.: Northwestern University Press, 1988). Hereafter this text is abbreviated as *Limited*.

7. Searle, *Pour réitérer les differences, réponse à Derrida* (Paris: Éditions de l'Eclat, 1991).

8. Jonathan Culler, *On Deconstruction: Theory and Criticism After Structuralism* (Ithaca: Cornell University Press, 1993).

9. Searle, "The Word Turned Upside Down," *New York Review of Books*, October 27, 1983.

10. Derrida, "Toward an Ethic of Discussion," afterword to *Limited*, 111–154.

11. "Reiterating," 198.

12. Ibid.

13. *Limited*, 29.

14. Ibid., 30–31.

15. Ibid., 35.

16. Ibid., 36. Literally "a more or less anonymous company," but the French phrase refers to a Limited Liability Company. See translator's note.

17. The French acronym SARL stands for Société Anonyme à Responsabilité Limitée. The American equivalent of this legal status is the Limited Liability Company (LLC). —Trans.

18. Ibid., 38.

19. Ibid.

20. Ibid., 38–39.

21. Ibid., 42.

22. Ibid., 43.

23. Even if Derrida leaves the seriousness of his argument in doubt for the entire length of his reply and plays with the potentially improbable nature of his controversy with Searle.

I. THE ITERATIVE AS THE REVERSE SIDE OF THE PERFORMATIVE

1. In order to preserve the distinction in French (linguistics, cf. Benveniste) between *énoncé* and *énonciation*, the latter is translated as "enunciation" whereas the former is rendered as "utterance." —Trans.

2. Paul Grice, "Meaning," in *Studies in the Way of Words* (Cambridge: Harvard University Press, 1991), 213–224.

3. Derrida, *Margins of Philosophy*, trans. Alan Bass (Chicago: University of Chicago Press, 1982), 307. Hereafter this text is abbreviated as *Margins*.

4. *Margins*, 309.

5. Ibid., my emphasis.

6. Ibid.

7. Ibid., my emphasis.

8. Ibid.

9. Ibid., 311.

10. Ibid.

11. Ibid.

12. Ibid.

13. Ibid.

14. Derrida, *Edmund Husserl's Origin of Geometry: An Introduction*, trans. John P. Leavey, Jr. (Lincoln: University of Nebraska Press, 1989).

15. The French verbal noun *vouloir-dire* (to want to say) is translated throughout as "intended meaning." This distinguishes it from *sens*, translated as "meaning," and *intention*, "intention." When used as a verb, the phrase will also be translated as "to mean to say." —Trans.

16. *Margins*, 312.

17. Ibid.

18. Ibid., 313.

19. Derrida, *Positions*, trans. Alan Bass (Chicago: University of Chicago Press, 1981), 22.

20. *Margins*, 313.

21. Ibid., 314.

22. Ibid., 315.

23. Ibid.

24. Ibid.

25. Ibid., 316.

26. Ibid. Translation slightly modified.

27. Derrida, *Positions* 47, my emphasis. Translator's Note: Translation modified: *Vouloir-dire* is rendered as "intended meaning," not simply "meaning"; *se tend* has been changed to "stretches itself" (Bass's "tenders itself" is unclear); and *essouf-flement* is given here as "breathlessness" to avoid confusion with the concept of the "exhaustion" of meaning in this book, that is, when a present intention is "exhausted" (exhaustively subsumed) in a meaningful utterance.

28. Which again brings Derrida closer to Grice, who also formed an indexical theory of communication.

29. *Margins*, 316.

30. Ibid.

31. Ibid., 317.

32. I am thinking here in particular of the important works of Jocelyn Benoist and the position he defends in Benoist, *Les limites de l'intentionalité* (Paris: Vrin, 2005).

33. Derrida, *Limited Inc*, trans. Samuel Weber (Evanston, Ill.: Northwestern University Press, 1988), 128, my emphasis. Hereafter this text is abbreviated as *Limited*.

34. Throughout, Derrida's neologism *différance* is translated as "differance." —Trans.

35. *Margins*, 317.

36. Ibid.

37. *HTW*, 23.

38. Ibid., 10.

39. Ibid., 16.

40. Austin's original comment on the Greek citation is omitted in the French translation: "i.e. 'my tongue swore to, but my heart (or mind or other backstage artiste) did not.'" —Trans.

41. Ibid., 9–10.

42. Ibid., 11.

43. *Margins*, 317.

44. Ibid.

45. The French *relève* here translates Hegel's *Aufhebung*. —Trans.

46. Ibid.

47. Ibid., 318.

48. Ibid.

49. Derrida, *Voice and Phenomenon*, trans. Leonard Lawlor (Evanston, Ill.: Northwestern University Press, 2011), 58. In many respects, Derridean repetition borrows its framework of mortification from the Freudian death drive. Cf. Derrida, *Résistances* (Paris: Galilee, 1996), 46–47.

50. Cf. Derrida, *Ulysses gramophone* (Paris: Galilee, 1987), 89–90.

51. Derrida's neologism *restance* affixes the suffix *-ance* from *resistance* to the word *reste*, "remainder." Alan Bass translates this word as "remaining," which annuls the neologism and the supplementary effects of the suffix *-ance* (also of course in *différance*). Derrida himself comments on the difficulty of translating his neologism *restance*, which Jeffrey Mehlman and Sam Weber render simply as "remainder," in *Limited*, 50–51. "Remaindrance" may not be more adequate to Derrida's meaning than "remainder," but as a neologism itself, it better reflects his style. —Trans.

52. *Margins*, p. 318. Translation modified.

53. Ibid., 318–319.

54. Ibid., 319.

55. Ibid.

56. Ibid.

57. Ibid.

58. On this point, see Derrida, "Form and Meaning: A Note on the Phenomenology of Language," in ibid., 155–173.

59. Ibid., 320.

60. Ibid.

61. Ibid., 321.

62. Undoubtedly more so in Searle than in Grice, for whom the pragmatic indication is communicated at the level of *perlocutionary* effects.

63. Cf. Stanley Cavell, *A Pitch of Philosophy: Autobiographical Exercises* (Cambridge: Harvard University Press, 1996), 79.

64. *Margins*, 322.

65. Derrida, *Writing and Difference*, trans. Alan Bass (Chicago: University of Chicago Press, 1978), 292.

66. *Margins*, 320.

67. Cavell, *A Pitch of Philosophy*, 80–81.

68. *Margins*, 321.

69. On this point see Derrida's strong response to Crépon et de Launay in Derrida, *La philosophie au risqué de la promesse* (Paris: Bayard, 2004).

70. *Margins*, 322.

71. Ibid.

72. *HTW*, 33.

73. Ibid., 34.

74. *Margins*, 322.

75. Ibid., 324.

76. Ibid., 324–325.

77. Ibid., 325.

78. Ibid.

79. Ibid.

80. Ibid., 326.

81. Ibid., 327. Derrida cites Austin here.

82. Ibid., 328.

83. Ibid., 329.

84. Ibid.

2. DO INTENTIONS DISSOLVE IN ITERATION?

1. John R. Searle, "Reiterating the Differences: A Reply to Derrida," *Glyph Review* 2 (1977): 199.

2. Ibid.

3. Ibid., 199–200.

4. Derrida, *Limited Inc*, trans. Samuel Weber (Evanston, Ill.: Northwestern University Press, 1988), 47. Hereafter this text is abbreviated as *Limited*.

5. Ibid., 48.

6. English in the original. —Trans.

7. Ibid, 49.

8. Ibid., 50.

9. "Reiterating," 200.

10. Ibid.

11. Ibid., 201.

12. Ibid.

13. Ibid.

14. Ibid.

15. John R. Searle, *Speech Acts: An Essay in the Philosophy of Language* (Cambridge: Cambridge University Press, 1969), 19.

16. Ibid.

17. Ibid.

18. Ibid., 21.

19. The French phrase "remonter en droit" is a play on the multiple meanings of the word "droit." It thus can mean both to "have the right" to return to intention and to return "directly" to intention (properly *tout droit à l'intention*). —Trans.

20. "Reiterating," 201–202, my emphasis.

21. *Limited*, 56.

22. To which Searle is attached, according to Derrida: "'metaphysical claim' does not signify here, or at least not in my mind, a futile or obscure speculation. It is for instance the structure described by Husserl (and I believe that I referred to this) in the *Logical Investigations,* following the movement of a rigorous phenomenological gesture. Searle is deeply indebted to him, whether he knows it, recognizes it, or not." Ibid., 120–121.

23. Ibid., 56.

24. Ibid., 57.

25. Ibid. Translation slightly modified.

26. Ibid., 58.

27. "Reiterating," 202.

28. Ibid.

29. Ibid., 201.

30. *Limited*, 72–73.

31. Searle, *Speech Acts*, 73–74.

32. Ibid., 75–76.

33. *Limited*, 81.

34. Searle, *Speech Acts*, 76, my emphasis.

35. *Limited*, 82.

36. Ibid., 68.

37. Ibid., 70.

38. The French word "répétition" means both "repetition" and "rehearsal." —Trans.

39. Derrida opposes the temporality of the "after-the-fact" or "belatedness" (French: *après-coup*; German: *Nachträglichkeit*) to the phenomenological temporality of the "present-now" in *Voice and the Phenomenon*. Derrida, *Voice and Phenomenon*, trans. Leonard Lawlor (Evanston, Ill.: Northwestern University Press, 2011).

40. Derrida, *Margins of Philosophy*, trans. Alan Bass (Chicago: University of Chicago Press, 1982), 18ff. Hereafter this text is abbreviated as *Margins*.

41. "Reiterating," 202.

42. *Limited*, 73.

43. Austin, "Three Ways of Spilling Ink," *Philosophical Review* 75 (1966): 427–440.

44. *Limited*, 73. Translation modified: the French text Moati cites reads "consciente de part en part, pleinement et actuellement présente." *Actuellement* should be rendered here in its temporal definition, hence "simultaneously."

   Derrida's translator Samuel Weber refers here to the Littré definition given in the preceding paragraph: "CONTRE-PIED 1. Hunting term. The trail followed by the prey and which the dogs, led astray, take instead of the new trail upon which the animal continues. To follow the *contre-pied* is to follow tracks in the wrong direction. 2. Fig. The contrary of something. 'People have taken precisely the *contre-pied* of the will.' La Fontaine." —Trans.

45. Ibid.
46. Ibid.
47. Ibid.
48. Ibid., 74.
49. Ibid.
50. Ibid.
51. Searle, *Speech Acts*, 58. Cited by Derrida in ibid., 74.
52. Searle, *Expression and Meaning* (Cambridge: Cambridge University Press, 1985). Hereafter this text is abbreviated as as *EM*.
53. Ibid., 62.
54. Ibid., 64.
55. Ibid., 65.
56. Ibid., 66.
57. Searle, *Speech Acts*, 79.
58. *EM*, 66.
59. The regime of conventional causality according to which I am engaged to keep my promise when I effectuate the act of promising. J. L. Austin, *How to Do Things with Words* (Oxford: Clarendon Press, 1962), 109ff.
60. "Reiterating," 206.
61. Ibid., 207.
62. Derrida, *Of Grammatology*, trans. Gayatri Chakravorty Spivak (Baltimore: Johns Hopkins University Press, 1976), 3–4.
63. "Let us not forget that 'iterability' does not signify simply, as Searle seems to think, repeatability of the same, but rather alterability of this same idealized in the singularity of the event, for instance, in this or that speech act." *Limited*, 119.

INDEX

Absence: of intentionality, in speech, 44; speech and, 77; writing and, 33, 77, 80

Alphabetic writing, 29

Arch writing, 83

Assertion, primacy of, 59–60

Ateleological acts, 64

Attridge, Derek, xii

Austin, John Langshaw, 102–3; citations, 67–70; on conflict between Derrida/Searle, J., 5–11; deconstruction approach for, 9; as disciple of Nietzsche, 55–64; felicity for, 18; first-person present indicative for, 72; illocutionary acts for, 55–57, 60–61, 63–64; infelicity for, 67; intentionality for, 45, 65–67; language as performative for, 56–57; metaphysics of presence for, 65–66; performative language for, 56; perlocutionary acts for, 55–56, 61, 63–64; pragmatic force for, 20; sensitivity to context for, 120; signifiers for, 66–67; theory of the performative, xv–xvi, 4; on truth/falsehood fetish, critique of, 17–18; truth

for, 57; utterances for, 68; *see also How to Do Things with Words*; Speech act theory

Authorship, in writing, 80

Badiou, Alain, xiii

Bass, Alan, 128n51

Bennington, Geoffrey, xii

Borkenau, Franz, xiii

Butler, Judith, xvi

Camus, Albert, xii

Cavell, Stanley, 57, 59

Citationality: intentionality and, 35, 48–55; of signs, 58; utterances and, 55

Citations: for Austin, 67–70; as concept, 98; definition of, 68; exclusion of, 69–70; multivalence of, 98; parasitism and, 112–16; use/mention distinction for, 97; writing and, 82

Cognition: consciousness and, 105; for Husserl, 26; perlocutionary acts and, 62

Communication: absence in, 33, 44, 77, 80; Derrida on, 16–17; dissemination from, 21–23; enunciation and, 13–16; through force, 16–21; gestural, 23–24;